Bruce Coville

WHO
WROTE
THAT?

Bruce Coville

Hal Marcovitz

Foreword by
Kyle Zimmer

A Haights Cross Communications Company ®

Philadelphia

CHELSEA HOUSE PUBLISHERS

VP, NEW PRODUCT DEVELOPMENT Sally Cheney
DIRECTOR OF PRODUCTION Kim Shinners
CREATIVE MANAGER Takeshi Takahashi
MANUFACTURING MANAGER Diann Grasse

STAFF FOR BRUCE COVILLE

EXECUTIVE EDITOR Matt Uhler
EDITORIAL ASSISTANT Sarah Sharpless
PRODUCTION EDITOR Noelle Nardone
PHOTO EDITOR Sarah Bloom
INTERIOR AND COVER DESIGNER Keith Trego
LAYOUT 21st Century Publishing and Communications, Inc.

http://www.chelseahouse.com

A Haights Cross Communications Company ®

First Printing

1 3 5 7 9 8 6 4 2

Library of Congress Cataloging-in-Publication Data

Marcovitz, Hal.
    Bruce Coville/Hal Marcovitz.
       p. cm.—(Who wrote that?)
    Includes bibliographical references and index.
    ISBN 0-7910-8656-9
1. Coville, Bruce—Juvenile literature. 2. Children's literature—Authorship—
Juvenile literature. 3. Authors, American—20th century—Biography—
Juvenile literature. I. Title. II. Series.
PS3553.O873Z76 2005
813'.54—dc22
                                                              2005008182

Table of Contents

FOREWORD BY
KYLE ZIMMER
PRESIDENT, FIRST BOOK

HUMANITY IS POWERED by stories. From our earliest days as thinking beings, we employed every available tool to tell each other stories. We danced, drew pictures on the walls of our caves, spoke, and sang. All of this extraordinary effort was designed to entertain, recount the news of the day, explain natural occurrences—and then gradually to build religious and cultural traditions and establish the common bonds and continuity that eventually formed civilizations. Stories are the most powerful force in the universe; they are the primary element that has distinguished our evolutionary path.

Our love of the story has not diminished with time. Enormous segments of societies are devoted to the art of storytelling. Book sales in the United States alone topped $26 billion last year; movie studios spend fortunes to create and promote stories; and the news industry is more pervasive in its presence than ever before.

There is no mystery to our fascination. Great stories are magic. They can introduce us to new cultures, or remind us of the nobility and failures of our own, inspire us to greatness or scare us to death; but above all, stories provide human insight on a level that is unavailable through any other source. In fact, stories connect each of us to the rest of humanity not just in our own time, but also throughout history.

This special magic of books is the greatest treasure that we can hand down from generation to generation. In fact, that spark in a child that comes from books became the motivation for the creation of my organization, First Book, a national literacy program with a simple mission: to provide new books to the most disadvantaged children. At present, First Book has been at work in hundreds of communities for over a decade. Every year children in need receive millions of books through our organization and millions more are provided through dedicated literacy institutions across the United States and around the world. In addition, groups of people dedicate themselves tirelessly to working with children to share reading and stories in every imaginable setting from schools to the streets. Of course, this Herculean effort serves many important goals. Literacy translates to productivity and employability in life and many other valid and even essential elements. But at the heart of this movement are people who love stories, love to read, and want desperately to ensure that no one misses the wonderful possibilities that reading provides.

When thinking about the importance of books, there is an overwhelming urge to cite the literary devotion of great minds. Some have written of the magnitude of the importance of literature. Amy Lowell, an American poet, captured the concept when she said, "Books are more than books. They are the life, the very heart and core of ages past, the reason why men lived and worked and died, the essence and quintessence of their lives." Others have spoken of their personal obsession with books, as in Thomas Jefferson's simple statement, "I live for books." But more compelling, perhaps, is the almost instinctive excitement in children for books and stories.

Throughout my years at First Book, I have heard truly extraordinary stories about the power of books in the lives of children. In one case, a homeless child, who had been bounced from one location to another, later resurfaced—and the only possession that he had fought to keep was the book he was given as part of a First Book distribution months earlier. More recently, I met a child who, upon receiving the book he wanted, flashed a big smile and said, "This is my big chance!" These snapshots reveal the true power of books and stories to give hope and change lives.

As these children grow up and continue to develop their love of reading, they will owe a profound debt to those volunteers who reached out to them—a debt that they may repay by reaching out to spark the next generation of readers. But there is a greater debt owed by all of us—a debt to the storytellers, the authors, who have bound us together, inspired our leaders, fueled our civilizations, and helped us put our children to sleep with their heads full of images and ideas.

WHO WROTE THAT? is a series of books dedicated to introducing us to a few of these incredible individuals. While we have almost always honored stories, we have not uniformly honored storytellers. In fact, some of the most important authors have toiled in complete obscurity throughout their lives or have been openly persecuted for the uncomfortable truths that they have laid before us. When confronted with the magnitude of their written work or perhaps the daily grind of our own, we can forget that writers are people. They struggle through the same daily indignities and dental appointments, and they experience the intense joy and bottomless despair that many of us do. Yet somehow they rise above it all to deliver a powerful thread that connects us all. It is a rare honor to have the opportunity that these books provide to share the lives of these extraordinary people. Enjoy.

In Bruce Coville's early novel, **The Monster's Ring,** *a boy named Russell discovers a way to turn himself into a monster for one day. Russell plans to punish a bully named Eddie. In the end, however, Russell (disguised as a monster) saves Eddie from being beaten up by even bigger bullies, and Russell and Eddie become friends.*

1

Mystery Lives!

WHEN BRUCE COVILLE worked as a teacher at Wetzel Road Elementary School in Liverpool, New York, he wrote a story about a young boy with the ability to turn himself into a monster. Coville had wanted to be a writer since he was 17 years old, but his work had gone unnoticed by publishers. Still, he enjoyed writing stories and reading them to his students.

Coville knew there was a problem with the story he had titled "Monster for a Day." Although the children seemed to enjoy the story—he read it to his classes every Halloween—he knew the story lacked a theme that would allow readers to connect with the main character. Coville finally realized that he had never given the boy a reason to want to change into a monster. Coville started looking around his classroom. He sought inspiration from his students and wondered which of them might want to become a monster. He asked himself what they would do if they had the power to turn themselves into a big, ugly, hairy beast.

It didn't take long for Coville to focus on a student named Russell. Coville noticed that Russell was constantly forced to endure the taunts of a bully. Of course, Coville said to himself, any little kid with a bully problem would love to turn into a monster—just for a day—so he could give the bully a taste of his own medicine. Coville rewrote the story and named his main character Russell. He also added a bully named Eddie. Finally, he based the story at Boardman Road Elementary School. Readers of the story could see that a number of characters at the fictional Boardman Road Elementary School bore a striking resemblance to real-life people at Coville's Wetzel Road Elementary School.

Later, Coville expanded the story into the book *The Monster's Ring*. It was the first in a series of books Coville would author in which the main characters enter a magic shop owned by the mysterious Mr. Elives. In *The Monster's Ring*, the main character, Russell, obtains a magical ring that enables him to turn into a monster by chanting this verse:

> Powers Dark and Powers Bright
> I call you now, as is my right.
> Unleash the magic of this ring,
> And change me to a monstrous thing![1]

Within minutes of uttering the chant, Russell grows horns, claws, and long tufts of brown and black fur. Does he pursue the bully named Eddie? At first, Russell has every intention of using his strength to pound on Eddie and make him suffer. Russell soon realizes, though, that fighting Eddie would give him little satisfaction. In the meantime, Russell learns Eddie's secret; that Eddie is the victim of bullying by teenagers. Indeed, just as Eddie is about to be beaten up by the older boys who corner him at the school's annual Halloween party, Russell swoops in on monster wings and saves him. In the end, Russell becomes friends with Eddie although he can't resist giving the bully a bit of a scare as well, just to teach him a lesson.

> Roaring with laughter, Russell flapped his wings and soared back into the night sky. He flew until he was out of Eddie's sight, then settled back beside a tree in Stearns Park. He was still chuckling. Frightening Eddie like that was the most satisfying thing he had ever done.[2]

"I think everyone gets bullied, which is one of the reasons I write about it a lot," Coville says, adding,

> I think kids like to read about that because they all experience it. Even bullies get bullied. There is always someone who is bigger that can push you around. I get mad at schools because they sometimes say when a kid is being bullied, "Oh, he'll just have to get used to it, because that's what life is like." But that's a lie. Adults do not go to work and get beat up on the job. And schools have a responsibility to protect children from bullies.[3]

The Monster's Ring was published in 1982. By then, Coville had achieved modest success writing picture books for young readers. His first book, *The Foolish Giant*, had been published in 1978. It was followed by a second book,

Although it might be hard to believe that this sweet looking boy on the tractor would grow up to be the author Bruce Coville, who takes delight in creating weird and magical monsters, ghosts, and goblins, it really is an early picture of Coville. Coville's grandfather, Leonard Chase, was a dairy farmer, and Coville spent many happy hours on his grandfather's farm.

Sarah's Unicorn. Both of these early books received high praise from critics, librarians, teachers, and other experts in children's literature. Still, Coville had not yet established himself as an influential writer for young people. Even after his first two books were published, Coville found it necessary to work as a teacher and later as a magazine editor to support his family. But his life would change dramatically after the publication of *The Monster's Ring*. The book proved enormously popular among critics as well as young readers. It served as the first story in a five-book series based on Mr. Elives's magic shop. And it propelled Coville into the ranks of America's most successful authors of fiction for young readers. The book's popularity enabled Coville to quit his job as a magazine editor and devote his life to writing scary stories for young people. Coville has said about *The Monster's Ring*,

> I always wanted to write this type of story—ever since I was nineteen. As you can probably tell, Halloween is my favorite holiday. I would always be in the library "haunting" the shelves looking for just the right book to read on Halloween. And I never found it. I found a lot of great books, but never just the right one. Really, what I was trying to do when I wrote *The Monster's Ring* was write the book that I wanted to read when I was eleven. And it's not perfect, either, which means I get to try again.[4]

Other books in the series include *Jeremy Thatcher, Dragon Hatcher*; *Jennifer Mudley's Toad*; *The Skull of Truth*; and *Juliet Dove, Queen of Love*. Each book has been praised by critics. Writing in *The New York Times Book Review*, critic Anne Jordan said of *The Monster's Ring*:

> Although this lively tale has a Halloween setting, it is more than just another story about that holiday. Halloween books tend to be so cute and unfrightening that they tend to cause cavities. While *The Monster's Ring* isn't frightening, neither is it cute. . . . It will appeal at any time to anyone who, like Russell, is "very fond of monsters."[5]

Each book in the series covers familiar and common themes: a young boy or girl stumbles into the magic shop, where they find a mysterious item. They believe the item they find will solve their troubles. In Russell's case, the item is the monster's ring. For Jeremy Thatcher, it's a dragon egg. Jennifer Mudley finds a talking toad. Charlie Eggleston

Did you know...

In one scene of *The Monster's Ring*, Russell uses his power to terrorize a classroom in Boardman Road Elementary School. He jumps onto a desk, swings his arms, roars and snarls, and succeeds in scaring everyone in the classroom—except Mrs. Brown, the teacher. She uses a broom to whack Russell across the backside. Bruce Coville based that scene on a story he would often tell his students at Wetzel Road Elementary School about his "half-mad twin brother," Igor, who lived four cellars down and only came out on his birthday, which also happened to be Halloween.

Coville, an accomplished actor, loves to play the role of Igor for friends and school students as well as around the house whenever the mood strikes him. Coville made Igor a character in his book *Goblins in the Castle*. Igor has a substantial role, assisting an 11-year-old orphan named William, who finds himself in a battle of wits against a group of goblins haunting Toad-in-a-Cage Castle. *"Goblins in the Castle* is a personal favorite of mine, partly because Igor was a character that I used to use when I was teaching," says Coville.

> In fact, I wrote the first version of the story because my kids and I had so much fun with the idea. That was back in 1977, and it took me a long time to find the right publisher, and also to solve some problems with the way I had first written the story. . . . The funny thing is, *Goblins in the Castle* is actually more like the kind of book I *started out* to write than anything else I have had published. So it is especially pleasing to me to find out that kids really like it.[*]

[*] *www.brucecoville.com/books/3-goblins.htm*

discovers a skull that never lies. And Juliet Dove, the main character in the final book in the series, finds a magical charm that makes her the center of attention of every male she meets. Instead of solving their problems, though, the magical items help each of the characters realize the truth about themselves. Each book contains elements of the supernatural as well as the type of humorous writing that Coville's fans expect of him.

And, of course, each book includes the character Mr. Elives, the gruff, white-haired owner of the magic shop. His withered brown skin reminds Russell of dried mushrooms. Still, his eyes "that glittered like black diamonds"[6] both frighten Russell and give him the feeling that the odd little man possesses a deep inner strength. Mr. Elives frightens all the heroes and heroines of the Magic Shop books, but at the same time he helps them find the special gifts that will change their lives. If readers of the Magic Shop books find themselves wondering how to pronounce Mr. Elives's name, Coville has some advice: "Just remember that 'Mystery lives!'"[7]

Bruce Coville lives in Syracuse, a city in upstate New York, only a few miles away from the village where he was born in 1950. The eldest of Jean and Arthur Coville's four children, young Bruce spent many carefree years in this area of upstate New York famous for its spooky tales and legends. Here we see the young Bruce Coville with his two proud parents, Jean and Arthur.

2

An Absolute Bookaholic

STORIES ABOUT GHOSTS and goblins were being told around Oswego County, New York, long before Bruce Coville was born there on May 16, 1950. Indeed, it is said that the ghosts of Basil Dunbar and George Fikes haunt the old Fort Ontario, a fort initially built by the British before the Revolutionary War. Both Dunbar and Fikes were soldiers stationed at the fort on the banks of Lake Ontario in the 1700s. Both men died under mysterious circumstances and are buried in the fort's cemetery. Little children play a game at George Fikes's grave. They believe Fikes's ghost will haunt the person they name if they jump over the dead soldier's grave while spitting and chanting. And just outside the fort, along some abandoned railroad tracks, it is said that the ghost of a Civil War soldier whose head was shot off by a cannonball wanders the tracks, searching for his head.

Oswego County and nearby towns are home to many other spooky stories. A lighthouse in the city of Oswego is rumored to be haunted by the spirits of three men who were lost during a storm. The dressing rooms of a theater in Oswego are believed to be haunted by the ghost of an old hobo who died in the basement. The junior high school in the town of Fulton is said to be haunted. Lights turn on and off by themselves, toilets flush by themselves, doors shut by themselves, and students report hearing mysterious voices in the hallways. The ghost of a woman dressed as a pilgrim has been seen wandering the road outside the village of Baldwinsville. South of Oswego County, in the city of Syracuse, New York, a ghost known as the "Woman in White" is thought to haunt the Landmark Theatre. Witnesses report seeing her image lingering quietly in the balcony section of the theatre.

Coville was born near the tiny village of Phoenix in Oswego County, just north of Syracuse. As a young boy, he was influenced not only by the Oswego area's wealth of spooky legends, but also the rural life of his farming community. Coville's father was not a farmer but his grandfather, Leonard Chase, owned a dairy farm. It was on his grandfather's farm that the young boy spent many happy hours:

I was raised in Phoenix, a small town in central New York. Actually, I lived well outside of town, around the corner from my grandparents' dairy farm, which was the site of my happiest childhood times. I still have fond memories of the huge barns with their mows and lofts, mysterious relics and jostling cattle. It was a wonderful place for a child to grow up. In addition to the farm, there was a swamp behind the house, and a rambling wood beyond that, both of which were conducive to all kinds of imaginative games. [8]

When Coville, the eldest of four children, wasn't helping his grandfather around the farm, he spent many carefree afternoons in the countryside near Phoenix. He climbed trees and swung on vines in the swamp near his house. At home, Coville and his brother Robert would cook up mysterious creations in the kitchen, such as a runny red cake frosting they pretended was blood, and then eat them. On summer nights, Coville and his friends from Phoenix would stargaze into the dark nights over Oswego County. They enjoyed making up stories about alien civilizations.

Coville's father, Arthur Coville, was a traveling salesman. His mother, Jean, worked as a secretary. Arthur Coville's mother had died when he was 3 years old and soon after, Arthur's father declared that he was unable to care for his young family. Arthur and his brother were raised by separate relatives who often feuded among themselves. Coville says, "In my father's case, it made him passionate about creating a good and stable home for his own kids, and working to make life better not only for us, but for as many kids as he could reach. That's one reason he became a volunteer in the scouting movement."[9]

While growing up in Phoenix, Coville recalls that late one Sunday afternoon in December the family piled into the car to head for Christmas dinner at his grandmother's house:

When we pulled out of the driveway, instead of heading for my grandmother's, my father turned the car in the other direction, heading for town. Our protests and questions were answered with the information that Dad had learned that the family of one of the boys in his Cub Scout pack was suffering hard times and not apt to have much of a Christmas meal. He had taken it into his head that this shouldn't be, and so before we went off to our own Christmas dinner, he insisted on going into town and buying a couple of boxes of groceries—everything it would take to make a solid, satisfying Christmas meal—and bringing them to the boy's family. That incident has become one of my most cherished Christmas memories, something that stands out when all the gifts and feasts have blended into a blur of getting and forgetting. With a single act Dad had shown us what Christmas was really all about, in a way that telling never had, or could.[10]

Neither of his parents seemed devoted to literature, but when Coville was a young boy, his father summoned him to the living room after dinner, sat him down, and read him an adventure from the Tom Swift series of books. The character of Tom Swift, hero of dozens of books dating back to 1910, was a boy genius and inventor whose adventures took him into remote corners of the globe, outer space, and deep under the sea. The book Arthur Coville selected to read to his son, *Tom Swift in the City of Gold*, featured the story of Tom's trip beneath the waters in a submarine. The book introduced Coville to the world of fantasy and science fiction. Coville has said,

Much of what went on at that time went on in my head, when I was reading, or thinking and dreaming about what I had read. I was an absolute bookaholic. My father had something to do with this. . . . He was a traveling salesman, a gruff but loving man who never displayed an overwhelming interest in books. But if anyone was to ask me what was the best thing he ever did for me I could reply without hesitation that he read me *Tom Swift in the City of Gold*. Why he happened to read this to me I was never quite certain, but it changed my life. One night after supper he took me into the living room, had me sit on his lap, and opened a thick, ugly brown book—this was the original Tom Swift—and proceeded to open a whole new world for me. I was enthralled, listened raptly, waited anxiously for the next night and the next, resented an intrusion, and reread the book several times later on my own. It was the only book I can ever remember him reading to me, but it changed my life. I was hooked on books. [11]

In addition to the *Tom Swift* books, Coville found many other favorite titles. He read *Mary Poppins* and *The Voyages of Dr. Doolittle* and the young readers' mysteries, featuring Nancy Drew and the Hardy Boys. He also enjoyed the books of Edgar Rice Burroughs, who wrote about the adventures of Tarzan, as well as John Carter, hero of a series of stories about Mars. Some of his other favorites were *The Wonderful Flight to the Mushroom Planet* by Eleanor Cameron, *The Black Stallion* by Walter Farley, *Penrod and Sam* by Booth Tarkington, and detective novels featuring Sir Arthur Conan Doyle's detective, Sherlock Holmes. And he read "zillions of comic books." [12] They were hardly high literature, to be sure, but they continued to make him hungry for fantasy and adventure. He adds: "My only real regret is the time I spent watching television, when I could have been reading instead." [13]

At school, Coville studied hard and earned good grades. "I was quite a good student," he recalls. "My worst subject was not writing, but handwriting. Sometimes people forget that they are different things. I was also lousy at gym." [14] Still, despite his devotion to schoolwork, he had trouble finding an outlet for his creative energies. That changed in the sixth grade, when Coville's teacher assigned him to write a short story. Unlike other writing assignments, which called on the students to write an essay on a particular topic, this assignment instructed the class to write freely on any subject they chose. Coville says:

> My sixth-grade teacher, Mrs. Crandall, had me write all year long. It was the first time I had had a teacher ask me to do much writing. They didn't have you write so much back in those days, which was dumb, because the only way you learn to write is by doing it. I failed at it all year long. But at the end of the year, she gave us a great assignment. We were going to write a story, and we got to work on it for a long period of time—two or three weeks. Not only that, they were all going to be read aloud, so we had an audience. And, this was the most important part, she didn't tell us what it was going to be about. Whatever we wrote had to come from inside. Every kid in the class did a great job, including me. And that was the first time I thought I would like to be a writer. Also, the fact that I love books made me want to be a writer, too.[15]

The story he wrote for Mrs. Crandall's class was about a lion and lamb who are raised on a farm that teaches animals to act in movies. When the train carrying them home from a job derails, the two animals must make their way home through the wilderness. He says, "I had so much fun writing the story, and was so pleased with it, that I got the idea of doing several stories about animals from that training farm. This is the first time I can remember having an idea for a book I wanted to write, though I never did write it."[16]

By the time Coville was 17 years old, he had made up his mind to become a writer. He started writing short stories, soon devoting himself to science fiction and fantasy:

I staggered through junior high and high school, victim to the forces that buffet everyone then—peer pressure and crushes, blossoming sexuality and social insecurity. I was not cut out for team sports—my coordination did not kick in until I was in my twenties—so that area of achievement was denied to me. But there were two teachers—one in eighth grade and one in tenth grade—who did something utterly invaluable for me. They told me I could write.

I don't want to indicate that I was unhappy during these years. I mostly enjoyed myself. I read incessantly, everything from the comic books that I still loved to Homer, Dante, and Shakespeare. I had my first crushes, and my first real girlfriend. In my junior year I ran for student council president. It was not a job I particularly wanted—we all knew who was going to win anyway, a popular and energetic girl who was right for the task. But the student council powers didn't want an election with only one candidate, so I was prevailed upon to run. I ran hard, deluded myself into thinking I might win, and was deeply pained when the inevitable loss occurred. [17]

Actually, there was one bright spot during his campaign for student council. While running for president, Coville asked a sophomore named Katherine Dietz, who was a very good artist, if she would design his campaign posters. "What she came up with was delightfully whimsical— probably too whimsical for someone running for student council president in high school, but just right for a picture book artist," he says.[18] Katherine became Coville's girlfriend and eventually his wife.

Coville was accepted to college at Duke University in North Carolina, which he attended during his freshman year. In his second year, he returned home, married Katherine, and enrolled at Harpur College, now part of the

State University of New York (SUNY) at Binghamton. He would switch schools once more before graduating, earning his degree at SUNY Oswego.

During the summer months, he held a variety of unusual jobs. He worked as a toy maker, a cookware salesman, an airfreight agent, and an assembly line worker, among others. He also found a most unusual job that would provide him with valuable experience as a writer of spooky stories. Coville's grandfather ran the cemetery in the town of Lysander, New York, and Coville found part-time employment digging graves. "In retrospect, it wasn't a bad job," says Coville.[19]

Certainly, his job at the cemetery gave him some measure of inspiration. For example, after digging a grave, he would often try it out for size, which he says helped him get over a natural fear of graveyards: "If you dig the hole yourself, if you lie down at the bottom of the grave . . . [the fear subsides]."[20]

Years later, Coville wrote a novel titled *The Ghost Wore Gray*. Two characters in the book, Nina and Chris, have to dig up an old grave. Coville, of course, had firsthand knowledge and was able to give his readers a particularly good insight into the chore of grave digging. "I knew what's involved," says Coville. "Write what you know."[21]

As for his writing, Coville found himself concentrating on children's stories. He had been inspired to write literature for young people mostly by Katherine, who was now providing illustrations for many of Coville's stories. "I thought if I wrote the stories, she could make pictures for them," he says. "We're married now, and that's what we do."[22] Indeed, while Coville was a busy author of short stories and novels, he was also the recipient of numerous rejection slips from publishers. It is very difficult for a new author to get noticed. Even the finest work goes unread by publishers, who are swamped with manuscripts and are often unwilling to take a chance on a new and unknown writer. "I call it getting the 'ugly baby' letter," says Coville. "They call the letter they send you the rejection slip. It's like getting a letter that says, 'Dear Mr. Coville, We have carefully examined photographs of your child, and boy do you have an ugly baby.' The story

Did you know...

The Landmark Theatre in Syracuse and its legend of the "Woman in White" served as inspiration for Bruce Coville's book, *The Ghost in the Third Row*, one of three books Coville wrote that featured the character of Nina Tanleven.

In *The Ghost in the Third Row*, sixth-grader Nina suffers a true case of stage fright while trying out for a play. She notices the ghost of a woman, wearing white, sitting in a third-row seat. Says Coville,

One of my favorite places in Syracuse, the city where I live, is a beautiful old theater known as "The Landmark." Many people believe quite firmly that this place is haunted. Once I was in a play at the Landmark and during rehearsals people would nudge me and whisper, "If you watch the balcony, you may see 'The Woman in White' go by." While I never saw Clarissa (that's her name) many people I knew claimed that they had.

I thought this was an interesting thing to base a story on. So when an editor named Ann Martin (yes, the very same person who later went on to create the Babysitter's Club series!) asked me to write a ghost story, the Landmark came to mind as a good place for the setting. I made up almost everything else—including, I am sorry to say, the brass elephant in the lobby. But the theater itself I described as accurately as I was able.[*]

* *www.brucecoville.com/books/3-thirdrow.htm*

is part of you, it's come from inside you, and when they say they don't want it, it hurts. But you can't let that stop you. Or you'll never get published." [23]

Before transferring to SUNY Oswego, Coville had decided to become a teacher. Certainly, he hadn't given up on the idea of writing. He chose SUNY Oswego because the school enabled him to major in education. "After all," he says, "there was no way I was going to make a living writing children's books right off the bat, I loved working with kids, and teaching would give me plenty of material for stories." [24]

By now, Coville and Katherine had started a family that would eventually include two sons, Orion and Adam, and a daughter, Cara. In 1974, just after graduation from SUNY Oswego, Coville found steady employment teaching at Wetzel Road Elementary School in Liverpool, New York, a few miles south of Phoenix. For the next seven years, Coville taught the second and fourth grades and used his spare time to write. He liked to read his stories to his students, and they gave him their opinions.

In the summer of 1975, he enrolled in a graduate class in children's literature at Syracuse University. One night Coville was talking with Katherine about his day while she sat with her sketchpad and drew as she listened:

> After a while she turned the pad around and said, "Write me a story about this guy." It was a picture of a forlorn looking giant, standing barefoot in a farmer's field. He had broken a fence by stepping on it, and the farmer, who only came up to his ankle, was berating him. What she had done in drawing the picture was give me the essence of a story—namely, the character. I knew by looking at it that he was big, that he got in trouble a lot, and that he was kindhearted. Otherwise, he would just have squashed the little guy yelling at him. [25]

High-school sweethearts Bruce and Katherine Coville have had a long history of collaboration on many of Bruce's most successful titles. Katherine's illustrations lend just the right dash of humor and life to Coville's books, and Coville credits his wife Katherine as his inspiration for writing books for young people. Here we see a recent picture taken of Katherine.

The storybook Coville and his wife created became *The Foolish Giant*. After working on the story and the illustrations for nearly three years, it was accepted by a publisher and published in 1978. Coville aimed the book at readers between the ages of 3 and 7. The text contains just 732 easy-to-read words. It is a story about Harry, a clumsy and not-too-bright giant. Other characters in the book include Harry's best friend, a young boy named Will Smith, and an evil wizard who intends to turn the villagers into stone toads. Harry means well, but he always manages to make the villagers angry. After he uproots the mayor's apple tree while picking flowers, Harry finds himself banished from the village.

> Wiping away his tears, Harry went home and packed. Then he moved to a cave far from town.
>
> But Will Smith followed him to see where he went, because he didn't want to lose his friend.
>
> When the wizard saw Harry go he rubbed his hands with glee. Now there was nothing to stop him from taking over the town.[26]

Harry returns just in time to stop the wizard's plans and becomes a hero. Katherine's humorous drawings show portly villagers, a bearded and pointy-headed wicked wizard, and a rumpled but lovable giant. *Publisher's Weekly*, the news magazine of the book industry, called *The Foolish Giant* "a treat for beginning readers and grand make-believe."[27]

Although Coville later concentrated on novels for a some-what older audience, *The Foolish Giant* would be the first of several picture books he authored for very young readers. A year after publishing *The Foolish Giant*, Coville and Katherine worked together on Coville's second picture book, *Sarah's Unicorn*. The book is about a young girl who battles an evil aunt with the help of a unicorn. *Publisher's Weekly* called the book an "effervescent story, make-believe at its best."[28] Later, Coville wrote a sequel to *Sarah's Unicorn* titled *Sarah and the Dragon*. Indeed, long after establishing himself as a novelist, Coville continued to author short books for beginning readers from time to time.

Sarah's Unicorn remains one of Coville's favorite books. The story tells of Sarah's friendship with a unicorn named Oakhorn. When Sarah's aunt, a wicked witch, finds out about their friendship, she is determined to rob the unicorn of his magic. "When you write a book, you always have something in your head that you're trying to create. What's in your head should be 'better' than you are actually capable of doing. I have never written a book that was as good as I wanted it to be, but *Sarah's Unicorn* is the one that came closest to the dream I had in my head."[29]

Coville says he intends his picture books to be nothing more than lighthearted reading for very young readers. He wants to make them laugh at a story while opening their eyes to the joys of reading. "I do not expect a child to read my picture books and suddenly discover the secret of the universe," says the author, adding:

> I do hope that something from my works will tuck itself away in the child's mind, ready to present itself as a piece of the puzzle on some future day when he or she is busy constructing a view of the world that will provide at least a [small amount] of hope and dignity. This may seem like a long-term goal and a minimal result for the work involved, but I am, after all, a teacher. This has always been our lot. We deal with a child for a year, pour our hearts and souls into his development, and then send him on his way with the scant hope that somehow, somebody, some little of what we have tried to do may present itself to him when it is needed. But this is idle speculation. The first and foremost job in writing is to tell a whacking good story. You just have to hope it might mean something before you're done.[30]

In addition to their printed form, Coville's stories are also available as audio books. Here we see the author at Todd Hobin Studios, where he records all of his books.

3

The Power of Myth

AS MANY PEOPLE know, the bear named Winnie-the-Pooh lives in the Hundred Acre Wood with his friends Piglet, Rabbit, Eeyore, Owl, Kanga, Roo, and Tigger. Winnie and the others find themselves falling into all sorts of misadventures. Luckily, their human friend Christopher Robin usually shows up to help them out of their jams. British author A.A. Milne wrote *Winnie-the-Pooh* and the other Pooh books as bedtime stories for his young son, Christopher Robin Milne. Pooh is based on Christopher's teddy bear. Milne drew his ideas for the other characters from the toys he found in Christopher's room.

Coville first read the stories of the Hundred Acre Wood when he was 17 years old. Katherine's mother, who was aware of Bruce's desire to be a writer, gave him a copy of *Winnie-the-Pooh*. He says,

> I suddenly knew that what I wanted to write was children's books—to give to other children the joy I got from books when I was young. This is the key to what I write now. I try with greater or lesser success, to make my stories the kinds of things that I would have enjoyed myself when I was young; to write the books I wanted to read, but never found. My writing works best when I remember the bookish child who adored reading and gear the work toward him. It falters when I forget him.[31]

Coville says he found himself enormously influenced by Milne's use of make-believe to tell the Pooh stories, particularly the way Milne has Christopher Robin interact with the make-believe creatures of the Hundred Acre Wood. Christopher Robin is a little boy, who talks to the make-believe creatures, plays games with them, and helps them solve their problems. In fact, the first Pooh story begins as Christopher Robin climbs down the stairs, dragging his teddy bear behind, asking his father for a bedtime story. The Pooh stories are about make-believe creatures, but there is always a relationship in Milne's stories between make-believe and the real world. Milne also told his stories with a generous amount of humor, a technique Coville would come to employ himself.

And so, when Coville writes, he tries to connect myth to the real world. His Magic Shop books are full of mythical figures and concepts—skulls that tell the truth, toads that talk, eggs that hatch into dragons, rings that turn boys into monsters—yet his characters are often ordinary young people who live in very real worlds. Yet, through Coville's words, his characters find themselves connected to mythical worlds. At the root of all Coville's books, readers find stories about young people dealing with very real, and very ordinary, problems.

"Myth is very important to me," Coville has said. He says his "books have firm roots in basic mythic patterns. Hopefully, the patterns do not intrude, but provide a structure and depth that enhances my work." [32] He adds that children can learn how to relate to real problems if they have been exposed to such issues first through mythical stories. In *The Monster's Ring*, for example, Russell resists the temptation to beat up Eddie and instead uses his monster powers to make friends with the bully. Coville believes children who read mythical stories grow up to be responsible adults. He says, "'Making sense' is a process that generally takes a lifetime and yet, sadly, is all too often never even begun. To utilize myth as a guide in this quest one must be familiar with its patterns and structures, a familiarity that is best gained from reading or hearing myth and its reconstructions from earliest childhood on." [33]

Of course, Milne was not the first author to employ myth as a storytelling device. The Winnie-the-Pooh stories first appeared in 1926. In 1904, a stage play written by British author J.M. Barrie was first performed, telling the story of an elfin boy named Peter Pan who refused to grow up. Lewis Carroll wrote *Alice's Adventures in Wonderland* a half-century before Milne authored the Pooh stories. Thousands of years earlier, the ancient Greeks wove mythical tales. They told stories of winged horses, women with snakes growing from their heads, one-eyed giants, and monsters that were half-bull and half-man. Indeed, every culture has legends that are passed on from generation to generation.

Two authors who helped Coville understand myth were Joseph Campbell and Robert Graves, both of whom examined the power of myth. Born in 1904, Campbell taught literature at Sarah Lawrence College in New York. In 1949, Campbell wrote *The Hero with a Thousand Faces*, which argued that all myths have common themes. According to Campbell, mythological stories always begin with the introduction of the hero and his call to adventure. Next, the reader is introduced to a character who is wiser than the hero and serves as a teacher or mentor. The hero then begins the adventure, which usually involves making a journey. Along the way, the hero makes friends and convinces them to accompany him on the journey. Often, they act as guides. There will be ordeals, temptations, dark nights, and setbacks along the way. During the journey, the hero also wrestles with problems of his own. He may ask himself whether he is worthy of other people's trust. He may fear that his own failings will doom the quest. Finally, there is a supreme showdown between the hero and an enemy. The hero wins, and after the fight, he returns home. Campbell believed every good myth shows how ordinary people have the power to respond to circumstances they encounter in real life. Indeed, Campbell's purpose was to show how myth reflects reality. Take out the dragons and winged horses, Campbell said, and what you find is an ordinary person making an ordinary journey. Coville says, "Over and over he makes the point that the mythic story is really the encapsulation of the human growth pattern. It's a way to track what we're supposed to do as we become adults."[34]

Robert Graves, born in 1895, was a poet, novelist, and historian. His books *The Greek Myths* and *The Hebrew Myths* also examine the relationship between myths and real-life events. In *The Hebrew Myths*, he argues that heroes are human and only with the help of God are they able to perform heroic deeds. Another Graves book, *The White Goddess*, points out the importance of female deities, or goddesses, in myth. "Campbell provided the male side of the story, Graves provided the female side," says Coville. "Together, they make a complete picture."[35] He adds, "The basic mythic pattern, old as man, deep as space, true as the sky, is represented in myriad forms and provides a way to make some sense of this muddled world of ours."[36]

The influence of Milne, Campbell, and Graves on Coville's work is evident in a series of stories he wrote about unicorns. Certainly, there is no more mythical creature than the unicorn—an imaginary creature represented as a horse with a long horn growing from its forehead. According to some myths, unicorns possess magic abilities. They can cure the sick, overcome evil powers, and make flowers bloom and rainbows appear in the sky. It is said that Alexander the Great once rode a unicorn and that Genghis Khan was persuaded by a unicorn not to attack India. Unicorns have long fascinated Coville, and his second published book, *Sarah's Unicorn*, involves a unicorn named Oakhorn. Later, Coville would write a series of novels called the Unicorn Chronicles, which started with his 1994 book *Into the Land of the Unicorns*.

The Unicorn Chronicles tell the story of Cara Diane, a young girl who employs the powers of a magical amulet, or charm, to pass from Earth into the Land of Luster, which is populated by all sorts of mythical creatures—the Dimblethum and the Squijum, to name two—as well as unicorns. Here is how Coville describes the unicorn Lightfoot:

> In shape, he was much like a horse, though somewhat smaller and more finely built. His hooves were cloven, like a goat's, rather than solid like those of a horse. Mane and flowing tail seemed spun of silver cloud and moonlight. From between his enormous dark eyes thrust a spiraled horn, three feet long at the least, that glowed as if lit from within.[37]

The books in the Unicorn Chronicles illustrate how Coville follows the rules of myth. In the first book, Cara is called to adventure by her grandmother, who urges her to leap from a church bell tower to escape an enemy, the Hunter. Cara makes the leap, using the magical amulet to enter Luster before she crashes into the street below. Once in Luster, she makes friends with the Dimblethum and the Squijum, finds a mentor in Lightfoot, and begins a journey to save the unicorns of Luster and learn the truth about her parents. Along the way there are breathless chases, a battle of wits against a dragon, and narrow escapes from evil creatures known as the "delvers."

> Lightfoot froze where he stood. She did the same until the delver guards leaped to their feet and, with a bloodcurdling scream, started after them.
>
> "On my back!" ordered Lightfoot.
>
> She obeyed without hesitation. No sooner had she scrambled onto his shoulders than he was off like a rocket, hurtling into the darkness. Hunched low over his shoulders, Cara wrapped her hands in his silky mane and prayed that she would be able to hold on. Branches whipped through the forest. Dark shapes rose before them, then vanished to the side as Lightfoot veered around them.[38]

The journey leads Cara and the others to a character named Grimwold, who tells them of a goddess—Beloved—who has vowed death to all unicorns, and how the unicorns escaped her wrath by fleeing from Earth to Luster. Now Cara's amulet has opened the gates between the two worlds, and the Hunters—men from Earth—are once again pursuing the unicorns. They are aided by the delvers, who are small demon-like creatures. The delvers have also sworn death to

Did you know...

Bruce Coville is often asked how he names his characters. Sometimes, he borrows names from friends, family members, or people he meets. Sometimes, he uses "naming dictionaries," which contain thousands of names. Young parents searching for names for their babies often use such dictionaries. "These are wonderfully useful for writers," Coville says of the naming dictionaries. "They offer many real but unusual names; even better, the good ones give the meaning of a name. No one else may know that you named your character 'Charles' because it means 'strong,' but I think knowing it yourself helps keep you on track as you are writing."[*]

Sometimes, Coville says, he will find names for his characters by "playing with sounds."[**] That is how he named the characters of the Squijum and the Dimblethum in *Into the Land of the Unicorns*. He says,

> I invented one creature who darts around and speaks in a high, squeaky voice, and another who is big and lumbering, with a deep, rumbling voice. I hope you can easily guess which name goes with which. Notice how the "um" sound repeats in *lumbering, rumbling,* and *Dimblethum*. While everyone knows that words are a writer's tools, I think they should be our toys as well. Sometimes, just playing around with words and sounds is the best way to create a memorable and appropriate name. I sit and make lists, letting the sounds roll out until the right one comes along; not too normal, not too weird, but just right to catch the character's unique personality.[***]

[*]   Bruce Coville. "The Name Game." *Writing* 25, no. 5 (February–March 2003).

[**] Bruce Coville's Interview Transcript, *www2.scholastic.com/teachers/ authorsandbooks/authorstudies/authorhome.jhtml;schsessionid= IADLNRYFM5CGKCQVAKUCFFAKCUBJYIV4?authorID=22& collateralID=5327&displayName=Interview+Transcript.*

[***] Bruce Coville. "The Name Game."

all unicorns. Cara's quest is to deliver the amulet to Arabella Skydancer, the queen of the unicorns.

Into the Land of the Unicorns is a mythical story, but Coville brings many elements of real life to Cara's adventure. At one point, her ally the Dimblethum—a large, furry bear-man—is captured and tortured by the delvers. Lightfoot suggests to Cara that she would do well to leave the Dimblethum behind so that she may continue her journey to the queen, but Cara insists on following the delvers in order to rescue the Dimblethum. She refuses to abandon the Dimblethum, as her parents abandoned her when she was a baby.

> Her mind was telling her that for the good of all they should flee with the amulet, taking it as far from this place as possible. Her heart was screaming that they could not leave their friend.
>
> In the end, her heart made the choice. Asking herself what her grandmother would do, she found herself thinking instead about her parents. The painful memory of the way they had abandoned her made it impossible for her to do the same to anyone else.[39]

Regardless of what the story may be about, humor is a very important element of Coville's fiction. *Into the Land of the Unicorns* is about a plot to murder all unicorns. There is violence in the book, some of it quite bloody. There is fear. But there is also a character known as the Squijum, which Coville describes as a cross between a monkey and a squirrel. "Talk later!" cried the Squijum. "Now now shake butts move feet hotcha get going!"[40]

Coville says he usually tries to make his sidekicks into humorous characters. He also tries to devise unusual languages and quirky speech patterns for them that set them apart from the main characters. A sidekick should be the main character's best friend, he says, but also a good friend to the reader.

The second book in the Unicorn Chronicles series, *Song of the Wanderer*, finds Cara continuing her journey. She must make her way through Luster to the unicorn queen, who asks Cara to bring back her grandmother Ivy so that old wounds can be healed. Believing that her grandmother, known to the unicorns as the "Wanderer," is on Earth, Cara must find a way back through the gate that opened at the beginning of the first book. A third book in the Unicorn Chronicles series, titled *The Last Hunt*, is planned for publication in 2005. In fact, Coville hopes to continue writing about unicorns for many years to come. "My plan is to keep writing about Luster for as long as I live, hopefully more rapidly than I have managed to date," he says. "Anyway, my ultimate goal and plan for the Unicorn Chronicles is do one book a year, for as long as people are interested . . . which I hope will be for a long, long time."[41]

Every book, whether it tells of unicorns or talking toads or truth-telling skulls, starts with an idea that bounces around in Coville's head until it finally takes form and is ready to be turned into a story. But where do the ideas come from? "I get my ideas from my unconscious mind, the part of the brain that dreams," says Coville.

> I probably don't have any more ideas than you do. But when I get one, I write it down. Everything you do, and every person you meet, could be the seed of an idea. I get ideas from reading nonfiction.[42]

A very important part of any Coville book is the world in which his characters reside and have their adventures. Sometimes, as in the case of the Magic Shop books, Coville chooses to base his story in a small town in America. He

Even before he was a well-known author, Coville the teacher got a kick out of bringing creatures and goblins to life for his students. Here we see a "bearded" and hunched over Coville, as a character who he says is his "half mad twin brother Igor." Half-brother Igor made yearly visits to Coville's classroom and, says Coville, was his "inspiration" for **Goblins in the Castle.**

describes streets and alleys and parks. Sometimes, the world is far different from most people's hometowns. For example, Luster is a land of deep green forests and meadows as well as snowcapped mountains. The flowers smell sweeter than any flowers grown on Earth. The water is sweet as well, made that way by unicorns who dip their horns into Luster's crystal-clear streams. When Cara drinks from the stream, it is "like drinking diamonds." [43] Says Coville, "I am slowly building that world in my head, and sometimes I am frustrated because it does not happen fast enough. But each thing I learn about it, each thing I invent that works, makes me love it more."[44]

Once Coville has envisioned the story and its characters, he begins to put words down on paper. Coville is known to be a very fast writer, sometimes turning out a novel-length book in a matter of weeks. Of course, some books take much longer. "Sometimes, the ideas just won't come," he says.

> *Skull of Truth* took me a long time to write. I worked on it, off and on, for over five years. Sometimes, the more trouble a book gives you, the better it is when you are finished. For example, *Song of the Wanderer* was a really hard book, and I didn't find its true ending until the ninth draft. But once I had it, I loved it.[45]

Typically, Coville says, it takes him about three months to write a book. "But every book has its own rhythm," he adds.

> I once wrote a 200-page book in ten days. Notice I said once! It never happened again. . . . Sometimes, you set a book aside and then come back to it. I'm usually working on more than one book at a time. But it's not hard to shift gears between them.[46]

When he writes, one technique Coville often employs is to end a chapter with a degree of suspense. He likes to convince the reader that something exciting will happen on the next page, so he will end a chapter with a hint of what will come next. For example, at the end of a chapter in *Into the Land of the Unicorns*, Coville describes how Lightfoot uses his horn to heal Cara's wound:

> The horn drew closer. Still she did not flinch, not even when it pressed against her shirt. Only when it pierced her flesh and began driving on toward her heart did she cry out.[47]

Certainly, it sounds as though Cara is about to suffer a fatal attack by the unicorn, but just by turning the page, readers learn that Lightfoot's horn is magical, and although Cara suffers a tingling sensation—"as if she were being shocked by a thousand tiny batteries"—Lightfoot has, in fact, healed her.[48] Says Coville,

> Sometimes, I write something that surprises me, just to make something scary happen, and I don't know what's going to happen next. Sometimes, I just go back and look over what I've written, and find the scariest spot, and make the chapter end right there. I do that because I know people tend to read to the end of a chapter, and when they close the book, you might not get them back unless you have them hooked.[49]

Coville is often asked by his readers how they can become writers. His first piece of advice to them is to start keeping a journal. When he was a college student, Coville read in a magazine that keeping a journal is a good way for people to learn how to write. "I tried to do everything that was supposed to be a good idea, and that was one of the things that was supposed to be a good idea," he says. "The college journal was an on-again, off-again thing, but I have extensive journals for the last twenty years."[50]

Indeed, Coville took the time to record his thoughts on a countless number of topics, from the books he read to the movies he saw to the vacations he enjoyed. At first, he would record his thoughts in longhand. Later, he switched to using a computer. Today, even though he doesn't keep a journal as often as he would like, Coville has nevertheless accumulated thousands of journal pages. Coville finds that whenever he is stuck and unable to think of a plot twist or can't adequately describe a character, or he needs to draw on a personal experience to add color to a story, he can reach into his journal files.

The journal is like a fishhook you can drop in your brain and pull out memories very efficiently. The sights and sounds and the smells are going to come rushing back to you . . . . I tell kids that there are a number of ugly truths about their lives, and one of them is that everything fades. If I'm with a group of fifth-graders, I'll say, "There's probably not one of you here who can tell me in detail what happened your first day of first grade, a very important day in your life, but it's all recorded in your brain. It's all registered there, and there is a way to save it and that's by keeping a journal. Journal keeping is a way of saving your life, saving yourself for yourself, a gift to give yourself, a gift to give yourself ten years later." I'll tell them about keeping a journal and using it like a fishhook to pull up images. I tell them that when I read a sentence in my journal it can bring up a whole day in my mind.[51]

Besides telling young writers to keep a journal, Coville also encourages them to read a lot. "Filling your brain with good stuff is an important part of the job," he says.[52] He also encourages them to start writing their own stories. "The way you learn to write is by writing, not by circling answers or filling in the blanks," he says. "It's the best answer there is. You learn to write by writing."[53] Coville says young writers should never give up. They should expect rejection and learn to live with it. Eventually, he says, people will recognize a good writer's talent.

He says, "To be a writer, you have to have enough self-confidence, self-assurance, or arrogance, depending on how people define it, to think that what you have to say is worth reading. Otherwise, how can you justify expecting people to spend their time with your words?"[54]

Ever since he was young, Bruce Coville has wondered if beings from other planets have ever visited Earth. It's no wonder then that Coville has written a number of books featuring extraterrestrials. My Teacher Is an Alien *sold over a million copies and established Coville as a major author of young people's fiction. Coville's other books that feature extraterrestrials include* Aliens Ate My Homework *and* Space Brat.

4

Visitors from Space

SPACE ALIENS IN Coville's universe come in all shapes and sizes. They are often green but occasionally purple and yellow. Sometimes, they are just two inches tall, sometimes they are three feet tall, and sometimes they are the size of humans.

Some of Coville's aliens are male, and some are female. Some are neither. Some have two legs, and some have four. Others have no legs at all. In Coville's 1993 book, *Aliens Ate My Homework*, one of the characters is Phillogenus esk Piemondum, or Phil for short. Phil is a potted plant that gets around thanks to small rockets mounted on the bottom of his pot. Phil is a member of the crew of the spaceship *Ferkel*, which has arrived on Earth in search of an intergalactic criminal named BKR. Phil may be a plant, but he is able to carry on conversations with his fellow crew members. The only problem is the words he speaks sound more like burps:

> Uncurling one of its dozens of tendrils, the plant pulled aside a leaf. With another tendril it pointed to a dark green pod hanging from one of its internal stems. "I suck air into the pod, then use it to burp out a sound."[55]

Coville has written more than 90 books. Many have been about space travel or visits to Earth by aliens. Indeed, space travel has long been a matter that has interested Coville, dating back to when he was a young boy living in rural New York State. On summer nights, Coville and his friends would stare into the dark night sky over his grandfather's farm. They would gaze at the stars and make up stories about what life must be like on other planets. As an adult, he continued to think a lot about life in space. He came to the conclusion that life must exist on other planets. "Absolutely there's life out there," he says. "I think it's less likely we'll find something than something else will find us. The question is whether they want to talk to us or not."[56]

Coville recalls watching the 1977 movie *Star Wars* and finding himself immensely impressed by the cantina scene. The scene is early in the film; Luke Skywalker and Obi-Wan Kenobi visit a cantina on the planet Tatooine to enlist the services of the pilot Han Solo. The cantina is populated by all sorts of bug-eyed, multicolored, and multishaped aliens speaking a variety of languages, but mostly enjoying each other's company. "That scene shows how the evolution of different creatures would be based on where they're from," Coville says.[57]

Since then, Coville has spent a lot of time wondering why aliens would visit Earth and what they would think of human culture. Would they be more advanced than people on Earth? Obviously, he says, because they have mastered interplanetary space travel and we haven't. Would they be puzzled by what they find here? Probably not, he says. "Any alien culture that could get here would be way ahead of us in technology and civilization," he notes. "The idea that they would come here and not understand anything about our culture is ridiculous. It is not very imaginative."[58]

Coville has taken that basic theme and transferred it into four highly successful series of books about aliens: the Space Brat series, My Teacher Is an Alien series, Sixth-Grade Alien series, and the Rod Allbright Alien Adventures books. He has also written or edited other books on adventures in space, including *Space Station Ice-3* and two anthologies of short stories titled *Bruce Coville's Book of Aliens* and *Bruce Coville's Book of Aliens II*.

His first book about a visitor from another planet was *My Teacher Is an Alien*, which was published in 1989. The book tells the story of three sixth-graders, Susan Simmons, Peter Thompson, and Duncan Dougal, who learn their substitute teacher is an alien. The alien, Mr. Smith, wears a disguise when he teaches class, but one day Susan follows her teacher home and sees him remove his mask, revealing a green-skinned, orange-eyed visitor from outer space.

> I started to shake. Whatever Mr. Smith was, I was pretty sure the face he was slowly uncovering wasn't anything that had been born on Earth. . . . Soon the handsome face of "Mr. Smith" was lying on the dressing table. The creature that

had been hidden underneath it began to massage his face—his real face. "Ahhh," he said. "What a relief!" He smiled at himself in the mirror, showing two rows of rounded purplish teeth.[59]

Susan learns that Mr. Smith's real name is Broxholm, and that he has plans to kidnap five Earth children and take them back to his own planet. She enlists Peter, the smartest boy at Kennituck Falls Elementary School, and Duncan, the school bully, to help her thwart the alien's plans and rescue Ms. Schwartz, their class's real teacher, whom Broxholm is holding captive in his attic.

My Teacher Is an Alien proved to be enormously successful. It sold more than a million copies and established Coville as one of America's most successful authors of young people's fiction. "At the time *My Teacher Is an Alien* was published, there wasn't much science fiction published for that age group," he says. "It wasn't believed kids read science fiction. That book really changed that opinion to some extent because it was so successful. No one expected it to take off the way it did."[60]

Coville thinks the title alone had a lot to do with the book's success. Obviously, he says, the title held a lot of appeal to many school students who firmly believe their teachers are, in reality, hideous green monsters. He says, "When *My Teacher Is an Alien* came out it took off like a rocket. It sold more copies in one year than my previous twenty books had sold in twelve years put together. It was clear that the title was part of that."[61]

Coville never intended *My Teacher Is an Alien* to turn into a series, but he would eventually find himself writing three more novels featuring Susan, Peter, and Duncan. Those adventures would not confine the characters to Kennituck Falls. The three young people would visit other worlds, observe other cultures, and experience other adventures. *My Teacher Is an Alien* is told from Susan's point of view. In the second book in the series, *My Teacher Fried My Brains*, Duncan undergoes a transformation from school bully to charming young man after his brains are fried. The third book, *My Teacher Glows in the Dark*, follows Peter as he encounters unusual alien customs while flying off in Broxholm's spaceship. The fourth book in the series, *My Teacher Flunked the Planet*, would turn out to be Coville's best-selling book of all time. Readers have bought more than 1.5 million copies.

My Teacher Flunked the Planet is more than just an adventure in space. In many of his books, Coville has his characters make comments about social issues, such as violence, cruelty, the high divorce rate, and war. In *My Teacher Is an Alien*, Peter and Susan discuss why Broxholm would want to kidnap five children. Perhaps, Peter suggests, they want to study young people to find out why adults fight so much.

> "Think about it," said Peter again. "Maybe these people are really peaceful. Maybe they've seen how much we fight, and they're afraid if we get much farther into space, we'll cause some huge war."[62]

In *My Teacher Flunked the Planet*, Peter, Susan, and Duncan have been entrusted with the job of convincing the Interplanetary Council to spare Earth from destruction. The book touches on many important social issues, including pollution, war, poverty, and hunger. Coville says he decided to use *My Teacher Flunked the Planet* to call attention to social ills after hearing a speech by Jonathan Kozol, a Harvard University-educated teacher, author, and activist who has devoted much of his life to improving the lives of people in poverty:

> I heard a speech, once, by Jonathan Kozol, who is a passionate advocate for social causes. That same day I was supposed to go see the book company that I had written *My Teacher Is an Alien* for. They wanted me to do more books, but I wasn't sure I wanted to. After listening to Mr. Kozol speak, I realized that the reason to write about aliens was so I could write about human craziness. I didn't realize, when I started, that there were going to be four books in the series. When I agreed to do more, it was going to be two—one for Duncan and one for Peter. But Peter's story was too big to fit in a single book, and I could feel it splitting even as I worked. It was distressing— I didn't want to write *two* more books at that point. But really, the story gave me no choice. I'm very proud of that book, but it was also very hard to write. The first draft of *My Teacher Is an Alien* took me only two weeks. It took six months to write *My Teacher Flunked the Planet*. And the research was heartbreaking.[63]

Some of Coville's readers believe he tends to give teachers a rough time in his books. After all, in *My Teacher Is an Alien*, the villain is a teacher. But Coville, a former teacher himself, says that if readers think about what he's written, they'll see his books actually support teachers. He says:

> If you read the books carefully, you will see that they are very teacher positive. In *My Teacher Is an Alien*, the real teacher, Ms. Schwartz, is a great teacher, and Susan is upset because she wants her back. In the final book, the kids talk about how important teachers are, how they are the hope of the world. How can you imagine that I have something against teachers?

Well, I do have something against "bad" teachers, because I do think teaching is the most important job in the world. But good teachers are worth their weight in gold, and should receive much more respect and honor than our culture generally gives them.[64]

Even with his decision to examine social issues, Coville's books remain, at their core, light adventure stories with a heavy dose of fun. In *Aliens Ate My Homework*, 12-year-old Rod Allbright is forced to act as a guide for a team of two-inch alien policemen. The leader of the squad, Grakker, is a little green man with an attitude. When Rod shrugs his shoulders in response to something Grakker has just told him, Grakker threatens to shoot him with his ray gun.

"You tried to throw me to the ground," he said, sounding offended. "Fortunately, the trained reflexes of a Friskan fighter are more than a match for such an obvious move."
    I started to ask what he meant, then realized my mistake. I suppose it should have been obvious: Never shrug while carrying a trigger-happy, paranoid alien on your shoulder.[65]

Rod Allbright is, by the way, the only character in Coville's fiction that Coville based on his own life. *Aliens Ate My Homework* was illustrated by Coville's wife Katherine, and she drew Rod to resemble Coville as a young boy. In the book, Rod is a bit pudgy and not very good in athletics, and does a lot of stumbling and bumping into things. "The sad truth is, I'm not much good at anything physical," Rod says. "That's why the other kids call me Rod the Clod."[66] And Rod's description of his grandfather's farm sounds very much like the farm young Coville often visited near Phoenix, New York.

Aliens Ate My Homework is another case of a title helping a book sell. Originally, the title of the book was to have been *Aliens Ate My Goldfish*. Says Coville, "But then I got to thinking about it, and I wondered if kids would like 'Homework' better. So I tried it out in schools when I was visiting. I would have kids vote on the titles. And they *always* preferred *Aliens Ate My Homework*."[67]

Aliens Ate My Homework was followed by three more space adventures featuring Rod Allbright. They include *I Left My Sneakers in Dimension X*, *The Search for Snout*, and *Aliens Stole My Body*.

In 1992, Coville wrote *Space Brat*, launching a third series about adventures of young people in space. The series, which includes five books, tells the story of a young inhabitant of the planet Splat named Blork. He throws terrible temper tantrums, thinking his spells of anger will help him get what he wants. Just as in real life, though, Blork learns that a bad temper turns people against him. Coville says:

It took *Space Brat* a long time to become a book. I wrote the first version of the story back in 1977, with the intention that it would be a picture book. My wife, Kathy, did a couple of hilarious sample illustrations. But the editor who had bought our first book, *The Foolish Giant*, turned it down, saying that she didn't think kids would be interested in reading about a noseless green humanoid from outer space. This was a few years before *E.T.*, about a noseless brown humanoid from outer space, became the biggest money-making film of all time, showing what she knew.

A few years later I rewrote it in chapter book form. None of the editors I was working with at the time wanted it then, either. It was too silly and strange for their tastes. Or, to use the current phrase, "They just didn't get it." Then, fourteen

Did you know...

As a boy, Bruce Coville was a devoted reader of comic books. He was such a fan that he soon started writing letters to comic book publishers, commenting on the stories.

"Comics—especially Marvel comics—were an essential part of my reading education," he says. "In time I became what was known as a Marvel letter hack, writing fan letters that were published on the letters page of various comic books. Not paid writing, but my first words to appear in print in a national publication."[*]

Coville continued to write letters to comic book publishers as a college student at Duke University in North Carolina. Eventually, Marvel contacted Coville and asked him to arrange a public speaking engagement for Stan Lee, creator of such comic book heroes as Spider-Man and the Incredible Hulk. "Would I be interested in bringing my hero in as a speaker? I nearly went out of my skin at the very thought," he recalls.

> Every year Duke had a major event called the "Symposium" where they explored a topic through numerous speeches and seminars. The topic for the 1968–1969 academic year was "Media." It fit perfectly! I plastered the campus with posters. We got good publicity in the campus paper. And we got a massive crowd. I was moderating the program, but I don't remember being nervous; I was probably too excited. Stan was a lively and engaging speaker and the event was a huge success.[**]

[*] Bruce Coville, *How I Got Here* [unpublished essay].
[**] Ibid.

years after I had first written the book, I sent it to my editor and she called me the very next morning to tell me she was buying it. I told her that if she was going to publish it, it would be good to get Kathy to illustrate it, since she had been in on the project from the beginning. I showed her some of Kathy's original drawings for the project, and she loved them. . . . This was our first major collaboration since *The Monster's Ring* in 1982. It was one of the most enjoyable projects we ever tackled. In fact, we probably have more fun working on the *Space Brat* books than anything else we do. [68]

In the sequel to *Space Brat*, titled *Space Brat 2: Blork's Evil Twin*, Blork reforms and loses his bad temper but has to endure the antics of his evil twin, Krolb. (Savvy readers may notice that Krolb is Blork spelled backwards.) Other books in the series find Blork battling his archenemy Squat, exploring the Planet of the Dips, and traveling back into prehistoric times, where he encounters a saber-toothed poodnoobie.

The Space Brat books show how much fun science fiction can truly be. And critics pointed out that readers of the Space Brat books—who are generally between the ages of 7 and 11—could learn some valuable lessons from Blork. In its review of *Space Brat*, *Publishers Weekly* said,

> Because the story is set in a foreign time and place, readers can easily perceive his obnoxious, offensive behavior and laugh at his misfortunes. The distance between Blork and young readers will help them confront their own misbehavior while preserving their dignity and confidence. As in the author's bestselling *My Teacher Is an Alien*, honest, straightforward language blends with a keen sense of humor.[69]

While *My Teacher Is an Alien* and Coville's other space-oriented books belong in the category of science fiction,

Coville admits that there is actually very little science in them. Coville says he considered going into detail about some of the science behind space travel in his books and concluded that his readers might not be ready for it. Indeed, the science of travel from star to star deals with the question of whether a man-made body can travel faster than the speed of light, which is 186,000 miles per second. In 1905, Albert Einstein, the great physicist and mathematician, proved in his Special Theory of Relativity that nothing can travel faster than speed of light, but over the years science fiction authors haven't let Einstein's law get in the way of their stories. They have concocted elaborate scenarios that seek to explain how a spaceship can travel quickly from star to star.

Coville says he simply decided that his readers are more interested in the story than the science. "I'm decent in science, but I don't have the engineering background essential to writing that kind of science fiction," he says. "When you talk about faster-than-light travel, you are at the very outer edges of science."[70]

In 1999, Coville published *I Was a Sixth Grade Alien*, which launched still another series about aliens, young people, and space travel. This series would eventually include a dozen books, all of which follow the adventures of sixth-grader Pleskit Meenom, a purple boy from the planet Hevi-Hevi, whose father is a diplomat with the Interplanetary Trading League. The League has decided to establish an embassy in Syracuse, New York. In the first book, readers meet Tim Tompkins, who describes himself "as a sixth-grade alien, the weirdest kid in the class"[71] until, of course, Pleskit shows up.

> It took a few seconds before I could really focus on the alien.
> He could easily have passed for human, except for three things:

1. He was totally purple.

2. He was totally bald.

3. He had a single stalk growing out of the top of his head. The stalk was about five inches long and thick as a pencil. From its top sprouted a walnut-sized knob.

He was wearing a long-sleeved white robe, decorated with strange designs around the cuffs and the bottom edge. It took another few seconds for me to realize the designs were shifting and changing, almost as if they were telling a story.[72]

A lot of what goes on the Sixth-Grade Alien series is based on what goes on in Syracuse, Coville's hometown. To provide illustrations for the books, Coville's publisher enlisted Tony Sansevero, a Syracuse artist. It was Sansevero's job to illustrate a totally purple, totally bald boy named Pleskit who happens to have a stalk growing out of his head. Sansevero developed the illustrations by convincing local residents to dress up as Hevi-Hevians. He then photographed them and drew illustrations based on the photographs. "I was very impressed because he really knew his stuff," Coville says. "He has in his blood this passion for science fiction and horror stuff."[73]

Coville used both Pleskit and Tim as narrators of *I Was a Sixth Grade Alien* as well as the subsequent books in the series. Each boy takes turns narrating the chapters, so readers receive an idea of what the world looks like through the eyes of a normal sixth-grade student and through the eyes of a sixth-grade student from the planet Hevi-Hevi. Here is an excerpt from Pleskit's side of the story:

Tim looked horrified and his voice sounded unusually squawky as he cried, "You kept your grandfather's brain after he died?"

Before I could answer, he closed his eyes. I could smell just the tiniest hint of embarrassment—the first time I realized that Earthlings have any ability to communicate by smell. When he opened his eyes again, I could tell he was trying to be calm. "That's very interesting," he said. "It is not a custom that we follow."[74]

In some of the Sixth Grade Alien books, Coville provides a glossary of Hevi-Hevian terms to help the readers in case they become confused while reading the text. The terms range from *febril gnurxis*, which is a sweet and nutritious breakfast cereal, to *pak-skwardles*, which is a high-protein, slightly sweet Hevi-Hevian snack made from fermented *dweezil* beans that have been stored in a cool dark space for at least three months, to *pinglies*, which are large, four-eyed amphibians that roam the subtropical *wampfields* of Hevi-Hevi. *Pinglies* are the size of cows but built like frogs and tend to travel in packs.

Anybody who can write a dozen books about a 12-year-old Hevi-Hevian's adventures on Earth is obviously having a lot of fun with the concept. Indeed, Coville says his only intention is to write a book that will be fun to read. He says, "I like reading about aliens myself. I mean, why write a book I wouldn't want to read? The only kid I know really, really, really well is me! Or, at least, the kid I used to be. So that's who I write books for."[75]

William Shakespeare (1564–1616), seen here in this portrait, is probably the greatest writer in the English language. Yet because his works are 400 years old, most young people find them very hard to read, let alone enjoy. Being a big fan of theater and of Shakespeare, Bruce Coville jumped at the chance to write a series of books that retell Shakespeare's plays into modern English that kids will find easy to understand.

5

Retelling Shakespeare

THESE ARE VERY bad times for Duncan, the king of Scotland. He has been forced to send an army to fight against a band of rebels, who are getting help from the king of Norway. Duncan's army puts down the uprising, but while returning from the battle one of Duncan's bravest generals, Macbeth, encounters three witches who tell him that he will one day be king. Their prediction prompts the ambitious Macbeth to murder Duncan.

That story sounds as though it could have been hatched by Coville, but it was not. The play *Macbeth* was written in 1606 by William Shakespeare, known as the greatest playwright in history. The plays of the English writer known as the "Bard" have been seen by theatergoers and read by students for generations. Indeed, few students in American schools can expect to graduate without being exposed to at least one of Shakespeare's 38 plays.

But since Shakespeare lived and worked 400 years ago, many students today find it difficult to follow his prose. He used a style of English spoken in sixteenth-century Great Britain under the reign of Queen Elizabeth I (a time known as the Elizabethan period). What's more, Shakespeare wrote his prose in what is known as blank verse, in which each line contains 10 syllables. In any event, since modern poets generally don't write in blank verse, students today aren't used to following that form of poetry. For example, when the witches tell Macbeth that he is destined to be king, he replies that to be king

> Stands not within the prospect of belief,
> No more than to be Cawdor. Say from whence
> You owe this strange intelligence? Or why
> Upon this blasted heath you stop our way
> With such prophetic greeting? Speak, I charge you.[76]

Enter Coville, who in 1992 commenced a project to retell Shakespeare's stories in easy-to-understand prose for students faced with the daunting job of reading the Bard's plays. Coville says the idea was first suggested to him by a book editor who had wanted for some time to produce a series of storybook volumes retelling Shakespeare for young readers. "It was all I could do to keep from throwing myself at the ground at her ankles saying, 'Me! Me! Please let me do it!' In one of the great acts of self-restraint in my life, I said, 'It's a great idea. If you get a chance, please keep me

Did you know...

Bruce Coville has long been a fan of the theater. He has acted and directed as well as written plays. His novel, *The Dragonslayers*, actually began life as a musical he wrote for his students to perform at Wetzel Road Elementary School. Over the years, productions of *The Dragonslayers* have been performed in Syracuse-area theaters.

To give his books as well as the books of other authors a theatrical presence, in 1999 Coville established Full Cast Audio, which produces audio versions of books for young readers. Most audio books are narrated by a single actor who assumes all the roles in the story. In Full Cast Audio, different actors portray the roles of the various characters. Coville's retelling of *Macbeth*, for example, features separate actors in the roles of Macbeth, Lady Macbeth, Duncan, Banquo, and the other characters.

Over the years, Full Cast Audio has produced spoken-word versions for more than 30 novels. For Full Cast Audio's production of Elizabeth Winthrop's novel *Red-Hot Rattoons*, a dozen actors were drafted for the book's more than 70 speaking roles. Actors from the Syracuse area assumed the roles. Winthrop appears on the recording as the narrator. The book tells the story about five young orphan rats who must make it in the world on their own. Ellen Myrick, a book editor and amateur actress who was invited to take on several minor roles in the production, said, "This is serious. It's fun, but there's also an earnest commitment to honor the author's words and bring them to life the best way possible."[*]

[*] Ellen Myrick. "The In-side Story: I Was a Rat at Full Cast Audio." *www.ingramlibrary.com/nwsltr/september03/ ILS_insidestory.html.*

in mind.' It was probably two or three years later when she called me."[77]

Coville's first effort was *The Tempest*, Shakespeare's comedy about a shipwreck, a magician named Prospero, a spirit of the wind named Ariel, and a beast called Caliban. Actually, he found the story quite similar to some of his own stories. "If you look at *The Tempest*, it is a fantasy. It's got a monster, a fairy, and a wizard," Coville has said.[78]

Since that book was published, he would go on to retell *Romeo and Juliet*, Shakespeare's well-known play about ill-fated lovers kept apart by feuding families; *Hamlet*, the tragedy about the prince of Denmark cheated out of his throne through the murder of his father; *A Midsummer Night's Dream*, Shakespeare's comedy about magic elves and mixed-up lovers; *Twelfth Night*, a romantic comedy about twins separated at birth; and *Macbeth*, a dark tragedy about murder, intrigue, and ambition in medieval Scotland.

"It remains one of the most popular—and most frequently performed—of all Shakespeare's works," Coville says of *Macbeth*. "A horrific tale of witches, murder, ghosts, and revenge, it deals poetically with many of the elements popular with young readers—which makes it a perfect avenue for introducing them to the Bard."[79] Indeed, *Macbeth* is full of murders as well as ghosts, witches, riddles, and mysterious predictions. It also contains some of the best-known phrases in the English language, such as "Out, damned spot!" and "Is this a dagger which I see before me?"[80]

Coville, who has a background in the theater, has occasionally found ways to introduce his readers to Shakespeare. In *The Skull of Truth*, Coville based the character of the talking skull on Yorick, the unfortunate court jester from *Hamlet* whose skull ends up in the prince's hands while Hamlet utters the famous line, "Alas, poor Yorick! I knew

Just as theatre productions require a full cast and production crew to produce a great play or show, so, too, do audio book productions to produce a first-rate reading of a book. Here we see author Coville (standing on left) with his good friend and business partner at Full Cast Audio Dan Bostick. Bostick is also a versatile actor. Seated is the late author, Paula Danziger.

him, Horatio; a fellow of infinite jest, of most excellent fancy."[81] Says Coville:

I spent some time flailing about in a search for the proper folkloric provenance for the skull before it struck me that there is one and only one well-known skull in all of western literature, and that is Yorick. Immediately the novel came to life for me. Yorick was a jester, of course, and so it made perfect sense for my skull to offer a torrent of wisecracks, bad jokes, and jesterly advice. One of the key scenes in the novel occurs when Yorick offers to show his life story to Charlie, the protagonist. Using a kind of magical sense-o-rama, he spirits Charlie back to 16th century Denmark, where he provides a back-story to the action of *Hamlet*. The scene culminates in the moment when Hamlet holds the skull and proclaims his famous "Alas, poor Yorick" lines, though the young reader experiences it all through Yorick's eyes—or more precisely, his eye sockets, since he is but bone by this point.[82]

Coville also made use of Shakespeare in his novel *Fortune's Journey*, which tells of a troupe of actors making their way west during the Gold Rush days. During his research, Coville learned that cowboys and cattle rustlers loved Shakespeare, and that traveling actors would give performances of the Bard's plays as they journeyed from town to town. In *Fortune's Journey*, Coville's characters constantly exchange Shakespearean dialogue and make references to the Bard's plays. For example, early in the book, the character of Jamie, a boarding house worker in a small prairie town, recites lines from Shakespeare's comedy *As You Like It* to prove to the troupe that he knows the play.

Aaron looked at Jamie angrily. "Why don't you stay out of this? Besides, how would you know?"

"Because I know the speech. It goes:

'All the world's a stage,

And all the men and women merely players.

> They have their exits and their entrances,
> And one man in his time plays many parts,
> His act being seven ages.'"[83]

"I had two reasons for threading Shakespearian material through these novels," says Coville. "First, it was enjoyable for me as a writer. Second, and more important, I was hoping that if I caught young readers with the thread of story I could also pique their interest in the plays those stories came from."[84]

To begin the project of retelling Shakespeare, Coville and his editor had to select the plays that would adapt best to the shorter format Coville had in mind:

> Obviously, the first question to ask if you're going to adapt one of the plays to the storybook format is, "Which one?" When working for young readers it is helpful to have one or more youthful characters they can identify with, as in *Romeo and Juliet*. Magic is always a big draw for young readers, so plays like *The Tempest* and *A Midsummer Night's Dream* work well. Kids also like the grim and the gory, so *Macbeth*, though lacking a youthful protagonist, has a certain appeal.[85]

Still, for Coville the challenge in retelling Shakespeare was to tell the stories in words children as young as seven could understand. While preparing to retell Shakespeare, Coville found that his first job was to familiarize himself with every line. He says:

> The first thing is to absorb the whole thing. I read it over and over again. I listen to it. I'll get the audiotape version and listen to it as I'm driving around. If there is a live version, I'll get the videotape and watch that version. I try to absorb the play, to get it into my focus before I regurgitate it.[86]

Coville also reads commentaries on the play written by scholars and critics so that he can better understand the messages Shakespeare intended to make in the play.

During this phase, Coville makes notes about the play. He creates a large chart, showing how many lines are in each scene. He then writes a short description of each scene, describing the main thrust of the action. He says:

> This done, I have a one or two page document that helps me see the structure of the play. More importantly, writing it out this way helps me find the "bones" of the play and gives me a better feel for its structure. At this stage I also begin to note lines that I want to use verbatim in the text, some simply because I love them, others because they are well-known enough that they are almost required for the adaptation.[87]

Finally, it comes time to retell Shakespeare. "At some point—usually when I can't avoid it any longer—I sit down and start to write," he says. "The hardest thing here is the first line; it seems I have to find that before I can get on with the story. That line may well change later. In fact, it usually does. But until I have it, I can't go on."[88] In *Macbeth*, the original first line is delivered by one of the witches. She says, "When shall we three meet again? In thunder, lightning or in rain?"[89] Next comes a brief exchange among the witches, who plan to meet Macbeth to deliver their prediction that he will be king of Scotland. In Coville's version, the first line of the story is changed to, "Thunder shook the skies over Scotland."[90] Clearly, Coville has set the dark scene of the play while using a minimum of words.

Coville's versions of each play run between 4,000 and 5,000 words, which are printed over 32 pages in a storybook format. That isn't much space to tell a story that when acted in its full length often takes more than three hours to perform. Coville says reducing Shakespeare into a storybook is a long and tedious process that takes several drafts to refine into the finished manuscript. Typically, Coville says, he will write too much, then send it to an editor to begin the process of shortening the story so that it will fit into the format. "The first manuscript I send the editor will be too long," he says.

> This is because, over the course of several of these projects, we've decided that it makes more sense for me to leave material in, so that we can discuss, negotiate, and argue our options than it does for me to hand in the tightest possible manuscript, which is my usual preference. It is during these negotiations with the editor that I may, regretfully, be forced to the conclusion that a character or subplot has to be discarded. Making these decisions can slow me down for some time, as they are very painful.[91]

And, of course, Coville must take Shakespeare's words and make them understandable to young readers who are not used to the vocabulary and expressions of a sixteenth-century Elizabethan dramatist. While there has to be some cutting and reorganizing of the work, for the most part Coville says that what the reader gets is the story that Shakespeare intended to tell. "I actually try not to rewrite," says Coville.

> What I'm trying to do is be true to the story as much as possible and in the very limited space I have, use as much of the language as possible. It's a translation of a story. What we're trying to do is make it not a stage version but a written version. We're writing not for the ear but for the eye. I know my Shakespeare books have been used anywhere from second-grade classes to college students. If you read my version before you read the play itself, you have a guide. I saw a

group of second-graders do a stage version of *A Midsummer Night's Dream* based on my retelling of the story. They were so into it.[92]

Early in *Macbeth*, there is a scene in which Macbeth's wife, Lady Macbeth, reads a letter from her husband and wonders whether he has the courage to kill the king. Lady Macbeth decides that she must talk her husband into carrying out the murder. Here is how William Shakespeare wrote the scene:

> . . . yet do I fear thy nature;
> It is too full o' the milk of human kindness
> To catch the nearest way. Thou wouldst be great,
> Art not without ambition, but without
> The illness should attend it. What thou wouldst highly,
> That wouldst thou holily; wouldst not play false,
> And yet wouldst wrongly win. . . .
> That I may pour my spirits in thine ear,
> And chastise with the valor of my tongue
> All that impedes thee from the golden round
> Which fate and metaphysical aid doth seem
> To have thee crown'd withal.[93]

And here is how Coville interpreted that scene for his readers:

Lady Macbeth pored over her husband's letter. The witches' prediction that he would be king set her mind churning. She paced her chamber for a long time, thinking of all that might be. "Yet I do fear your nature, my husband," she muttered. "It is too full of the milk of human kindness for you to catch the nearest way. I shall have to urge thee on, to do what must be done."[94]

Certainly, both versions tell of Lady Macbeth's evil intentions. In Coville's version, Shakespeare's key phrase—that Macbeth "is too full of the milk of human kindness"—is preserved. Coville says, "I've learned little ways to squeeze in more and more of the language, but keep it accessible. Both my editor and I are aware of what we are doing. We want to be respectful to the source and to the audience. We work really hard on these books."[95]

Macbeth carries out the murder and seizes the crown. Next, he orders his friend Banquo killed, fearing that another prediction of the witches—that Banquo will be the father of a ruler—will come true. Banquo's ghost returns to haunt Macbeth, who confesses his crime to the spirit. Now, fearing that a Scottish nobleman named Macduff aims to have him killed, Macbeth orders Macduff's murder. The killers fail to find Macduff, but they slay his wife and children. Lady Macbeth, feeling pangs of guilt over the turn of events, is troubled by her conscience. Looking at her hands, she is convinced they are covered with King Duncan's blood. As hard as she tries, Lady Macbeth is unable to wash the blood from her hands. Shakespeare wrote:

> Out, damned spot! Out I say! One: two: why,
> then 'tis time to do't. Hell is murky. Fie, my
> lord, fie! A soldier, and afeard? What need we
> fear who knows it, when none can call our power to
> account? Yet who would have thought the old man
> to have had so much blood in him?
>
> . . . .
>
> Here's the smell of the blood still. All the
> perfumes of Arabia will not sweeten this little
> hand. Oh, Oh, Oh![96]

In Coville's version, Lady Macbeth said:

> Out, damned spot—out I say! Who would have thought the
> old man to have had so much blood in him? What, will these
> hands never be clean? Here's the smell of blood still. Oh, all
> the perfumes of Arabia will not sweeten this little hand.[97]

Finally, Macduff and Duncan's son Malcolm join forces
and attack Macbeth's castle. Macduff slays Macbeth, and
Malcolm takes back the throne. No question, there is a lot of
evil and bloodletting in the play, but that is how Shakespeare
wrote it. In a story published in the *Charleston Gazette*,
writer Dawn Miller said she read Coville's version of
Macbeth to a group of fourth graders. "The students loved
it," she wrote. "They marveled at the evil, dominating Lady
Macbeth. They discussed Macbeth's culpability. Was he to
blame? Or were the crimes his wife's fault?"[98] And in the
magazine *Teaching Pre K-8*, educator Phyllis Fantauzzo
wrote:

> I am sure you agree that plowing through 16th-century original
> Shakespearean plays is difficult for adults, let along children.
> Even though the stories are entrancing, the language can be
> confusing to readers who, unfortunately, can get intimidated and
> turned off by classic literature forever. Bruce Coville's retelling
> of *Macbeth* may be just what you've been looking for to get
> your students interested in Shakespeare.[99]

According to Coville, Shakespeare's plays have a lot of
appeal to young readers because they are, at their heart,
simply good stories. He says:

> Indeed, it is stories that children long for, and it is "Story" that is
> the entry point for many people to the pleasures of Shakespeare.

I think it is sometimes hard for Shakespeare scholars and enthusiasts, having swum for years in the sweet ocean of his poetry, to recall the thrill of having one of the plays unfold as story—to remember experiencing it for the first time and being stirred by that ancient question: What happens next?

If you tell your tale well enough, children, especially, will want to hear it over and over, in a multitude of forms, and will follow it into new venues—venues into which they might not otherwise have ventured, such as Shakespeare in text or performance. It may, indeed, be true that the stories are the least part of Shakespeare, but they are also the armature on which all else depends. The hope I hold in doing my retellings is that with an early and pleasurable experience of Shakespeare a child will be able to find his or her way past what I call "the curse of greatness"—the bizarre idea generated by our culture that because Shakespeare's plays are great that they are also too hard for the average mortal to understand, and that there is more work than pleasure involved in experiencing them, whether on the page or on the stage.[100]

Whether working with his wife Katherine who illustrates some of his work, or with friend Jane Yolen as coauthor on the book, Armageddon Summer, *Bruce Coville's approach to his work often involves collaboration. Here we see Coville with friend Angela Peterson, who composed the music for the show "The Dragonslayers."*

6

Describing the End of the World

IN THE LATE 1980s and early 1990s, as the calendar headed toward the year 2000—the start of the third millennium—several self-styled experts on Biblical prophecy predicted that the world would soon end in a fiery storm. They told their followers that only true believers in Jesus Christ would be saved. They based their predictions on their studies of the Bible, insisting that modern-day events closely mirrored conditions described in the Holy Scriptures necessary for the return of Christ.

Some of the predictions about the end of the world were prompted by fears that all the computers in the world would suddenly shut down at midnight on January 1, 2000, or, as the date was more popularly known, Y2K. By 1999, the "Millennium Bug" was a big concern to many people. Most records kept by governments, businesses, and others are kept in computer files. Some people predicted mass chaos if every computer in the world locked up, all at the same moment. Many people feared the worst and stockpiled food, water, and other supplies, believing that the Millennium Bug would prevent their ability to obtain the basic necessities for life.

The so-called experts who predicted the end of the world told of the coming "Armageddon"—the final battle on Earth between good and evil. Some of the experts in Biblical prophecy even went so far as to set a date for Armageddon. One of the most well-known of the predictors was Harold Camping, a California-based religious radio commentator who wrote a best-selling book titled *1994?* in which he suggested that Christ would return sometime between September 6 and September 27 in 1994.

The prediction by Camping and other millennialists caught the attention of author Jane Yolen. She recalls,

> I read about some millennialist group or another declaring that the world was going to end on a certain date and at a specific time. These news stories pop up every year, and not just when we are heading downhill toward a millennium. The old storyteller's "what-if" kicked in. And I began noodling— that's a writer's technical term for thinking about a subject as a possible book project. I asked myself, "What if a teenage girl is dragged to a mountain top by her family under the influence of a religious millennialist cult and there meets a teenage boy also brought up the mountain kicking and screaming? Would there be a summer camp romance? Would they be Romeo and Juliet, dying at the end? Or would the

whole cult go down, like the Titanic? Would the world end? Or would it begin?" I thought a lot about writing the book. But this was long before I really considered myself a novelist. Most of the time I am a short form writer. Long novels tend to give me nosebleeds! So I was not ready to attempt such a big and difficult story. Because big and difficult it threatened to be. It had to deal with love, death, matters of faith, family dynamics—and the end of the world.[101]

Since Yolen did not want to tackle the book on her own, she hoped to convince another author to cowrite the book with her. She made only one call to her friend Bruce Coville. He quickly accepted her offer to collaborate on the novel, which would soon be titled *Armageddon Summer*. Says Coville of the project,

> It immediately appealed to me partly because I thought she would be fun to work with, but also because I had been fascinated by the religious impulses in this country for a few decades. Upstate New York was called the "burned over" district by religious scholars because there were so many waves of religious revivalism that passed over here. People were spiritually burned out. This whole story about the world ending at a certain date certainly came up as we approached the year 2000, but it has happened over and over again. You see it happening every ten years. People claim to know when the end is coming.[102]

For Coville, *Armageddon Summer* would mark a significant departure from his usual brand of fiction. In *Armageddon Summer*, there would be no unicorns, space aliens, or ghosts showing up to haunt castles. He had occasionally written straight dramatic fiction—*Fortune's Journey*, for example—

but *Armageddon Summer* was intended to be a very ambitious book examining a serious topic that had come to dominate the news.

Yolen and Coville developed a story about a 13-year-old girl named Marina and a 16-year-old boy named Jed whose families are drawn into believing the world will end on July 27, 2000. Marina's mother and Jed's father are members of the Church of the Believers, a fringe group headed by a well-spoken and dynamic leader named the Reverend Beelson. The pastor convinces his church members to follow him to a camp atop Mount Weeupcut in Massachusetts, where he says they will survive Armageddon. Members of the church leave their homes and even their disbelieving spouses to head to the mountain where they make camp to wait out the storm. Early in the book, readers are aware that Jed simply doesn't believe in Beelson's prediction. He has made the trip only so that he can protect his father. Marina wants to believe in the Armageddon, but she finds herself full of doubts.

I wandered until it was time for evening Service, as if by walking I could solve my growing ambivalence, or maybe God would give me a hint as to how to feel, or what to believe.

A signal

A sign.

A burning bush.

Or maybe one of the grown-ups could put it to me plainly. Why *we* should be saved and not anyone else. Not my pen pal in Japan, not my grandparents, not my dad.

What made us better? What made us Angels? Was it as simple a thing as belief?

Then what would happen if I stopped believing altogether?[103]

Marina and Jed eventually meet and fall in love, but the book is far from just a simple romance. Yolen and Coville explore the theme of religious fanaticism—how people can have intense devotion to a cause or idea that may be irrational. They describe the deterioration of both Jed and Marina's families. Marina's mother walks out on her husband because he refuses to believe in Beelson's prediction. Jed's mother abandons her family; his distraught father finds comfort in joining Beelson's flock. Once on the mountain, Marina's mother turns over the responsibility for caring for the family's five young children to Marina because she is wrapped up in preparing for Armageddon and has no time for them. Jed watches in horror as his father starts carrying a gun after Beelson assigns him to protect the gates of the camp so no outsiders can enter for protection once the end arrives. Both Jed and Marina come to realize that Beelson and their parents have abandoned the Christian values they had once believed in— charity, goodwill, and the responsibility to help others. Jed says:

> Reverend Beelson offered the longest prayer I had ever heard. It went on and on about the Wickedness of the World (you could just hear the capital letters in his voice), the New Day to Come, the Fellowship of the Believers, and how Those Who Scorned Us Now would regret it when they were Washed Away in the Tides of Fire.
>
> He seemed to take a lot of pleasure in the idea, which didn't strike me as being entirely Christian, at least not as I had been taught to understand the word.[104]

Coville says:

> I was raised in a Christian family. The moral values that were instilled in me and by my church still survive. I found them at

odds with what this subset of Christianity practices. And that's what they are, a subset. It is a subset of a subset that presumes to speak for all of Christianity. That's what the Y2K thing was all about—it was the focal point for all the floating anxiety that comes up in a culture at the turn of the millennium. If we didn't have Y2K somebody would have had to invent it. It became the perfect way to focus all those fears.[105]

Coville and Yolen are not the only authors who have chosen the end of the world as a literary topic. Indeed, for years authors have speculated on how the world might end. For the most part, those stories had nothing to do with the final battle between good and evil and instead were concocted by writers who wanted to alert people to the horrors of war. The 1957 novel, *On the Beach*, written by Nevil Shute, is required reading in many high school literature classes. It follows a submarine crew as they search for signs of life in a world obliterated by nuclear war.

As Coville and Yolen were writing their account of the end of times, two other authors were also creating their own series of stories based on Armageddon. The Left Behind series was written in two versions—one for adults, the other for teens. Authors Jerry B. Jenkins and Tim LaHaye based their stories on the premise that the people left behind on Earth must survive horrific and bloody battles, terrible acts of nature, and supernatural events all orchestrated by Satan. Left Behind: The Kids, a series written for teen readers, follows four young people as they struggle to survive the end of times. There is no question that the Left Behind books held an enormous amount of appeal for readers. More than 60 million copies of the adult and teen versions were sold.

Coville says *Armageddon Summer*, although not written in response to the Left Behind books, nevertheless tried to offer young people a different vision of the year 2000—that it would turn out to be nothing more than a normal year in the history of the Earth and that what people had to truly fear was not Armageddon, but the millennialist cults that preached a coming doomsday. Coville adds,

> This was written before the Left Behind series really took off. They weren't on our minds when we were working on that book, but it was to try to examine what happens when you get drawn into one of these cultish things. What is the thought process? What are you believing to take on this idea? The greatest challenge in writing the book was to make the leader of the cult not a cartoon. It would have been very easy to make him a caricature, but I really wanted to make him a fleshed out, rounded character because there has to be something very attractive about somebody like that or the cult can't form to begin with.[106]

Indeed, readers of *Armageddon Summer* can see that Beelson possesses a large degree of personal charisma. At first, Jed fears the minister but soon comes to admire him—although never to the point where he becomes a Believer. When Beelson discovers that Jed has smuggled a laptop computer into the camp, in violation of the rules, the minister finds it in his heart to forgive the boy and even allows him to keep the computer. Jed is overwhelmed by Beelson's kindness and concludes that Beelson isn't such a bad guy, after all. "I wanted to believe Beelson was a nut. But if he was, then how could he sit and talk in such a calm, gentle and convincing way?"[107]

Jed's opinion of the minister changes as the hour of Armageddon approaches and events on top of Mount Weeupcut become darker and more sinister. Beelson orders his followers to surround the camp with an electrified fence. Armed guards are posted at the gates. Outside the camp, dozens of would-be Believers gather, hoping to gain entrance so they can be saved as well. And then, in the final few hours before the date set by Beelson for the start of Armageddon, chaos erupts in the camp. The latecomers storm through the gates. A riot breaks out. Gunshots explode into the crowd. A fire destroys the cabin serving as the Believers' church. To Jed and Marina, it seems Armageddon has arrived, but not the way Beelson predicted.

Armageddon Summer proved a new experience for both Coville and Yolen. At 266 pages, it was the longest piece of fiction attempted by Yolen. For Coville, it represented an effort to write fiction for older teens, members of an age group too old to enjoy *Aliens Ate My Homework* or *The Monster's Ring*. For both authors it was an experience in collaboration—the job of working together on a single project. They had to combine their voices into a single manuscript, ironing out details such as the plot, the pace of the action, and the roles of major and minor characters. Some of those issues weren't so easily worked out. For example, Coville usually writes a very detailed outline for his novels and sticks to it as he writes. Yolen, on the other hand, is more willing to stray from her outlines.

Yolen and Coville elected to write the story as it unfolds through the eyes of Marina and Jed. Each of the two main characters alternate as the narrator of each chapter. The first chapter is narrated by Marina, the second by Jed, the third by Marina, and so on. It was decided that Yolen would write Marina's chapters, while Coville would write as Jed's voice.

With such details finally worked out, the two authors got down to putting their words on paper. In 1995, Coville and Yolen were scheduled to serve on the faculty of a writers' conference in Washington State. That gave them the opportunity to be together for several days. When not lecturing student writers, they worked on the book, swapping chapters and comparing notes. By the end of the conference, they had finished the first 10 chapters of *Armageddon Summer*.

"Jane would write a chapter, hand it to me, and I would respond with a chapter of my own the next day," says Coville. "They were short chapters, and what we were really

Did you know...

Bruce Coville credits Helen Buckley, a children's book author and teacher at the State University of New York at Oswego, with helping him become an author. While attending SUNY Oswego as a student, Coville confided to Buckley his ambition to write for young readers, and Buckley invited him to show her some of his work. He says,

> She agreed to read a book that I was working on, which was far and away above the requirements of her job. When she gave it back she told me it was good and she would read the rest of it if I finished it. That in itself was sufficient to spur me through to the end. Later I got to take a writing class from her.
>
> During one session Helen put a box on the table and told us to write a story about it. Most people wrote about what was inside the box. But my brain twisted in a different direction; I thought, what if you had the box but could never find out what was inside. I wrote a short story called "The Box" about a boy who is given the box by an angel, who asks him to take care of it for him. The story remains my own favorite piece out of everything I have written. After Helen's death, her husband sent me the box, which I keep above my desk. It is one of my proudest possessions.*

* Bruce Coville, *How I Got Here* [unpublished essay].

trying to do was find the voices for our characters."[108] At the conclusion of the conference, Coville returned to Syracuse while Yolen went home to western Massachusetts. They planned to continue on as before, e-mailing each other their finished chapters. Yolen and Coville discovered, however, that they worked at dramatically different paces. Coville tends to write slowly while Yolen keeps a fast pace. Coville found that e-mailing chapters back and forth interrupted the rhythm of the project. Coville said:

> I still desperately wanted to do the book. Finally we decided that the best way to get me back in harness would be for me to drive to Jane's house—she lives about five hours east of me—where we would spend a week working together on the book.
>
> In January of 1996 I went to Jane's, and we rolled up our sleeves and went to work. It was some of the most intense writing I've ever done. A couple of things fueled the process. The first is that Jane and I are ever so "slightly" competitive. The second is that we were devoting ourselves completely to this project, shutting out the outside world and moving into our own world on top of the mountain where the Believers had gone to await the end of the world.
>
> If our first swapping of chapters and ideas had been about building our characters, now we were trying to build that world, to visualize the place where the story would take place, and work out the logistics of how this band of Believers would actually organize their camp to wait for the end of the world.
>
> Underlying the question of logistics was an even more interesting and challenging question, that of psychology. What would it be like to believe—to really believe—that the world was about to end, and only you and the tiny group of people around you, would survive the holocaust? What were these people thinking? What were they feeling? More

specifically, what were our two young protagonists—one a believer, one not—thinking and feeling while all this was going on? We wrangled considerably over the details.[109]

Yolen wrote in her third-floor attic, which she had converted into a home office. Coville set up his laptop computer in a spare bedroom. "The stairs got worn as we alternately tromped up and down," says Yolen.

> Lunch became sandwiches with plot talk. Breakfast was cereal with characterization. Even on our necessary long walk-breaks we talked about the book. In some ways, our writing times brought out the very best in me—invigorated and challenged me. I found myself energized and stimulated and pushed to the limit. By the end of our sessions my fingers were worn down to the nubs.[110]

Coville adds, "And we wrote. In my case I turned out as much in four days as I sometimes do in a month. It was exhilarating."[111]

After a week of fast-paced writing, Coville returned home to Syracuse. The book was not yet finished, but Coville had other projects that required his attention. For several months, neither author found the opportunity to work on *Armageddon Summer*. In January 1997, Coville returned to Yolen's house and they delved into the project. According to Coville, "Usually, writers put in a few hours of intense writing in a day. But with the end in sight, with the ferment of ideas driving us on, swapping chapters as we wrote, revising each other's text, passing them back for rewrites and new drafts, we put in marathon days, including one day when we wrote for fourteen hours. And we had a book."[112]

Armageddon Summer was published in 1998 to widespread acclaim. Reviewing the book, *Publishers Weekly*

The well-known author Jane Yolen (pictured here) has been a longtime friend of Bruce Coville, so it's not surprising that Yolen called on Coville to coauthor a book with her. The book, Armageddon Summer, *marked a real departure for Coville, however, with its absence of unicorns, extraterrestrials, ghosts, and other weird characters and creatures that feature so prominently in Coville's other works.*

said, "The action builds smoothly and steadily. Providing action, romance and a provocative message, this novel could well get teens talking."[113] The novel won several awards, including selection by the American Library Association as one of its Best Books for Young Adults.

On the cover of *Armageddon Summer*, readers will notice that Yolen's name is listed first. Coville says that was an easy decision to make, given the fact that Yolen had, after all, come up with the idea for the book. But Coville says Yolen's original idea was to write a short book, no more than 100 pages, that would tell a simple story about a boy and a girl on a mountain, caught up in the madness of the millennium. Coville says he saw that the book had the capability to deliver a strong message about the influence of cults and the wrongness of using organized religion to stir up people's fears. He says,

Jane is a source of wisdom and comfort to me on many matters, but on one matter in this book I was quite confident she was wrong. Early on she said to me she thought it was going to be a short book, maybe a little over a hundred pages, and that it wouldn't take that long for us to write it. I think I knew better than she did herself at that point the strength of the idea that she had come up with.

Part of that strength was in what the story let us talk about. For I think that the last taboo in children's books these days, and one that needs desperately to be shattered, is religion. Right now it seems we have two ways of dealing with religion in stories for young people. We either proselytize, primarily in stories published by specifically Christian or Jewish presses, or we pretend that the subject simply does not exist. This leaves a strange void in our books for young readers, and is no more real or sensible than all of us choosing to write stories in which no one has cars. Besides, we should not ignore the reality of children's lives, which is that most of them do indeed think about matters of faith, of the spirit. They do wrestle with what their relationship to organized religion is going to be. More so than many adults, for they are still alive to wonder. If we refuse to acknowledge this in our books for young readers, we leave a glaring hole in our work, and deny the truth of their own lives.[114]

Like many popular authors in America, Bruce Coville has seen some of his books threatened with censorship. A number of conservative religious groups believe that Coville's fantasy books promote and glorify such practices as Satanism and witchcraft. Books by such authors as Judy Blume, Shel Silverstein, and J.K. Rowling—to name a few—have been subject to this same kind of censorship.

7

Fighting Censorship

COVILLE HAD HIS first experience with censorship when he was getting ready to graduate from high school. At the time, the Vietnam War was raging. Young people were loudly protesting the war. They burned their draft cards, marched in demonstrations, and fled to Canada rather than submit to the draft. Meanwhile, civil rights leader Martin Luther King, Jr., had been killed by an assassin. Senator Robert F. Kennedy, who pledged to end American involvement in Vietnam, was also assassinated as he campaigned for the presidency.

Coville was very moved by the events of 1968 and aimed to speak out on the injustices of the war and the assassinations of King and Kennedy. He had been selected salutatorian of his high school class, which meant that his grades were among the highest scored by any student that year. The role of the salutatorian is to deliver a speech at graduation exercises. Coville noted that this developed into an interesting situation.

I wrote a passionate speech about social justice inspired by all that was going on at the time. But when I submitted it to the advisor, I was told I could not deliver it. My first experience with censorship!

I wrote another speech. It was approved, but I had no intention of delivering it. This was the age of protest, and I was going to protest the attempt to keep me from making the speech I had earned the right to give. For a time I planned on doing something very dramatic: I was going to hold up the speech that had been approved, tear it up, talk about what had happened, then give the first speech that I had written. I figured I would be hustled off the stage before I could finish, but I wanted to let everyone know what was going on. But as I thought about it, I realized something that became one of my guiding principles: I had to make a choice between making what might have been an emotionally satisfying scene or trying to accomplish what I really wanted, which was to make the speech I had first written, telling people what I thought and believed.

In the end, I simply went to the podium with my original speech and delivered that rather than the one that had been approved. I don't know for sure what would have happened if I had tried to make a big deal out of it. I do know that by doing it this way I didn't give anyone an excuse to try to stop me; if the advisor or the principal had tried, they would have been seen as the ones causing a disruption. After the ceremony one of the other senior class advisors, who had not been aware of the censorship attempt, sought me out and pumped my hand, saying, "That was a hell of a speech!"[115]

Coville had won his first battle against censorship. As he became a best-selling author, though, some of his books would face censorship challenges, the outcome of which would not always be to Coville's liking.

Each year, hundreds of books face censorship fights. Typically, a teacher assigns the book to students or a librarian orders it for the school library's shelves. The book may focus on an issue that parents or other members of the community find objectionable. They raise concerns with the school board, which may order the book removed from the classroom or library, or may impose rules that limit its availability to students. Every fall, the American Library Association sponsors Banned Books Week to call attention to censorship. In 2003, the association reported that 458 books faced censorship battles. Among the most challenged books that year were books in the Harry Potter series, authored by J.K. Rowling, because some people objected to the supernatural themes of the series, and the books in the Alice series, written by Phyllis Reynolds Naylor, because of the author's sexual content and use of offensive language. Sometimes, people object to books that are regarded as classics. John Steinbeck's book *Of Mice and Men* (1937), which can be found in middle school and high school English classes throughout America, made the association's list of "Ten Most Challenged Books of 2003" because of the author's use of offensive language.

Many times, the people who object to what they believe is offensive material in literature are members of fundamentalist Christian churches. They often lead very conservative lifestyles and warn their children against reading material that uses offensive language or describes lifestyles different from their own. They are particularly sensitive about portrayals of religious images. Coville first faced censorship of one of his books in 1993, when a devoutly religious couple in the rural community of Carroll, Iowa, objected to *Jeremy Thatcher, Dragon Hatcher*, contending that the book contained references to Satan worship and witchcraft. The parents, David and Cindy Peterson, asked Carroll Community Schools Superintendent David Proctor to remove Coville's book from the libraries of Fairview Elementary and Carroll Middle schools, which their children attended. A committee of Carroll parents, teachers, and students had already decided, by a margin of five votes to three, to remove the book but the final decision was left in the hands of the superintendent. "Their concern is that it's creating an unnecessary interest in the occult," Proctor told a reporter.[116] The book, meanwhile, was defended by the school librarian as well as a teacher in Carroll.

Proctor said he read *Jeremy Thatcher, Dragon Hatcher* twice and couldn't find a single reference to Satan. He said the Petersons objected specifically to Coville's use of the colors red, silver, and black and the symbols of stars and moons, which he said have been associated by some people with the occult. The Petersons complained about Jeremy feeding chicken livers to the dragon, suggesting that Satanists are known to eat the body parts of animals during their rituals. Also, the Petersons pointed to some 25 pages in which Jeremy communicates telepathically with the dragon Taimat. "That's their point, that it's kind of a subconscious way to get into children's minds," said the superintendent.[117]

When Coville learned that parents suggested that *Jeremy Thatcher, Dragon Hatcher* contained references to devil worship, he bristled. "Even Santa Claus is 'Satan' spelled inside out, so his cover is blown," said Coville. "There are people who believe this stuff, and I suppose that is their right. But if we are going to let them control what all children read, you might as well lock the library door and throw away the key right now."[118]

After assessing the complaints of the Petersons and hearing from Coville, who defended the book, Proctor decided the objections were groundless and permitted *Jeremy Thatcher, Dragon Hatcher* to remain on the shelves of the school district libraries. Despite the ruling, the Petersons believed they had won something of a victory. David Peterson, the pastor of a Christian church in Carroll, told a reporter, "We feel we have accomplished part of our goal . . . to encourage parents to exercise their rights to be aware of what their children are reading. Not everything children want to read is healthy for them. That's why God gave children parents, to guide them."[119]

Jeremy Thatcher, Dragon Hatcher may have found its way back to the Carroll library shelves, but Coville realized that the stir caused over the book could lead to a much more serious form of censorship. He says,

> It initiates what is called "gray censorship." Gray censorship is the censorship you cannot track. When *Jeremy Thatcher* was taken off the shelves in Iowa, there was a fair amount of news coverage of it. One of the letters I got was from a school superintendent who said, "This is probably good for you because it will sell more books." My response was I guarantee that

I'll get a momentary bump [in sales] in that town, but for a hundred miles around that town there will be principals who lean over to librarians and whisper in their ears, "Don't give me a problem like that." There were librarians who didn't need that whisper. They just said, "I don't need that problem in my school." They would quietly make the book disappear or make their buying decisions based on that. Even when you prevail in a censorship battle, the gray censorship it initiates is untrackable and [harmful]. [120]

Two years later, another Coville book would face a similar test. In Elizabethtown, Pennsylvania, parents and a school board member objected to *My Teacher is an Alien* because of the book's use of the phrase "Oh my god" as well as references to menstruation. A school committee reviewed the book and found no reason to remove it from the library, but the committee suggested that teachers use discretion when reading the book out loud and change "Oh my god" to "Oh my gosh" if they felt their students would feel more comfortable with the latter term.

Then, in 2004, parents in the Iowa town of Solon raised complaints about a book titled *Am I Blue?: Coming Out from the Silence*. The book, which was first published in 1994, is an anthology of short stories about gay teenagers. Coville contributed the story "Am I Blue?" which book editor Marion Dane Bauer selected as the title story for the anthology.

The story begins as the school bully, Butch Carrigan, beats up the narrator, whom Butch suspects is gay. The narrator explains that he isn't sure of his own sexuality and that he is in a questioning period of his life. As the narrator picks himself out of the mud, he is visited by an effeminate man named Melvin, who identifies himself as the narrator's fairy godfather. Melvin tells the narrator that he is entitled to three

"My writing works best," Bruce Coville says, *"when I remember the bookish child who adored reading and gear the work toward him. It falters when I forget him . . . The first and foremost job in writing is to tell a whacking good story. You just have to hope it might mean something before you're done."*

wishes. Together, they decide that one of the narrator's wishes will be for him to see gay people in shades of blue. And not only that, but long-time and devout homosexuals will be dark blue, while young people who are in a questioning phase like that of the narrator will be light blue.

> It was like seeing the world through new eyes. Most of the people looked just the same as always, of course. But Mr. Alwain, the fat guy who ran the grocery story, looked like a giant blueberry—which surprised me because he was married and had three kids. On the other hand Ms. Thorndyke, the librarian, who everyone *knew* was a lesbian, didn't have a trace of blue on her.
>
> "Can't tell without the spell," said Melvin. "Straights are helpless at it. They're always assuming someone is or isn't for all the wrong reasons." [121]

When the narrator looks at his own skin, he sees a light shade of blue. And Melvin informs the boy that Butch Carrigan is "blue as a summer sky." [122] According to Coville, a decade ago, positive stories about young gay people were a rarity in literature. In the past, he says, authors could write about young gays but only if they pointed out that the lifestyle is not proper. "You could be sympathetic to a gay character but somebody had to die so that everybody knew it was a bad idea," he says. [123]

In Solon, eighth-grade teacher Sue Protheroe assigned *Am I Blue?: Coming Out from the Silence* to her English students. Soon, seven parents filed complaints with the school district. One of the parents, Doug Singkofer, told a reporter, "My most significant concern is why, for material that is controversial, was there no notification sent out to the parents?" [124] Indeed, Singkofer said he was not aware that his daughter had read *Am I Blue?: Coming Out from the Silence* until he overheard her talking about the book with a friend. In their formal complaint to the school district, Singkofer and his wife Lynn wrote, "The material directly contradicts and undermines the beliefs and teachings of our faith. It introduces a very adult and mature subject to an inappropriately young audience. It is likely to introduce sexual confusion to a group of children who are just becoming sexually aware." [125]

Protheroe defended the book, explaining that she had used *Am I Blue?: Coming Out from the Silence* off and on for some five years as an example of a modern fairy tale. "I'm trying to teach tolerance and respect for all people, and I can't do that and ignore a whole group of people. Furthermore, I wouldn't present a curriculum that ignored women or African-Americans or Hispanics. How can I possibly teach my students to embrace diversity if I systematically exclude an entire group from my literature?" [126] She added, "This isn't about whether homosexuality is right or wrong. It's about kids learning to think for themselves." [127]

Even so, Solon Schools Superintendent Brad Manard said the school board would have to act on the complaints and decide whether Protheroe should be ordered not to use the book in her classes. After reviewing the issue for two weeks, the school board ruled in Protheroe's favor. Board member Ben Pardini told the parents they could appeal the Solon decision to state authorities in Des Moines "if your goal out there is to take your personal views and instill them in your children and also force them on all children." [128]

Again, fiction by Coville had been called into question and, again, he had weathered the storm. Still, Coville remains concerned about the gray censorship that may follow *Am I Blue?: Coming Out from the Silence* throughout the country. And sadly, Coville believes that with the government of the United States becoming more and more conservative, authors will long have to deal with censorship issues. Indeed, Coville sees America slowly creeping toward the atmosphere of the 1950s, an era when communist hunters aimed to wipe out all literature they perceived—rightly or wrongly—to be sympathetic to communism.

Did you know...

In 2005, Bruce Coville hopes to publish a novel for young readers based on the poem "Thrymskvitha," which relates the story of an ancient Norse myth that tells of the theft of Thor's hammer. In Norse myth, Thor is the god of thunder. He is a heroic figure, often using his great strength for the good of mankind. His hammer, the Mjolnir, strikes with the power of lightning and always returns to Thor's hand after he throws it. According to the poem, the hammer is stolen by King Thrym, who threatens to use it unless the gods give him Freya as a wife. Freya is the Norse goddess of beauty. In the process of retrieving his hammer, Thor dresses up as Freya and visits King Thrym. Coville has titled his novel *Thor's Wedding Day*. Says Coville,

> I first became aware of the story in other retellings of Norse myths, and thought it would make a great picture book. I sold the picture book version about five or six years ago, but soon after the publisher decided that picture book retellings of folk tales and myths were no longer profitable, so the project went on hold. My editor kept saying, essentially, "We'll figure out what to do with it someday." We were batting around some ideas, and decided that maybe the way to solve the problem was for me to try it as a novel.[*]

[*] Hal Marcovitz's interview with Bruce Coville, December 13, 2004.

Coville says, "In 'Am I Blue?' there is a story about tolerance, which a certain subset of our culture has a big problem with. I had hoped that once we passed the 2000 millennium madness, that would fade, but I no longer feel as confident about that because we are re-entering the period that reminds me very much of the 1950s."[129]

As for parents and others who would suggest they know what type of literature is best for their children, Coville has a simple answer: Perhaps they would do well to let the children themselves decide. He says,

> Sometimes kids do a much better job of telling the difference between fantasy and reality than a group of adults. *Jeremy Thatcher, Dragon Hatcher* has been taken off the shelf in one school district for what they called "Satanic content"—the presence of the dragon, the chicken livers, the silver gleam, and the use of black and red colors here and there in the book. It went back on the shelf after a protracted discussion and once I got involved in the issue. . . . I can only say that, for me, fantasy fiction sometimes is a way of telling an amusing and engaging story and fantasy fiction sometimes addresses important issues at a deeper level than realistic fiction does.[130]

Using the words of C.S. Lewis, author of the Chronicles of Narnia series of fantasy adventures, Coville says, "Sometimes the best way to tell the truth is to tell a fairy tale."[131]

1 Bruce Coville, *The Monster's Ring* (New York: Harcourt Books, 2002), 12.

2 Ibid., 75.

3 Bruce Coville's Interview Transcript, *www2.scholastic.com/teachers/authorsandbooks/authorstudies/authorhome.jhtml; schsessionid=IADLNRYFM5CGK CQVAKUCFFAKCUBJYIV4? authorID=22&collateralID= 5327&displayName=Interview+ Transcript.*

4 Between the Lines: Interview with Bruce Coville, *www. harcourtbooks.com/authorinterviews/bookinterview_Coville.asp.*

5 Anne Jordan, "The Monster's Ring," *New York Times Book Review*, October 31, 1982, 27.

6 Coville, *The Monster's Ring*, 5.

7 Ibid., 105.

8 Quoted in Robin Tallis, ed., "Bruce Coville," *Something About the Author*, vol. 118 (Farmington Hills, MN: Gale Group, 2001), 36.

9 Bruce Coville, *How I Got Here* [unpublished essay].

10 Ibid.

11 Quoted in Robin Tallis, ed., "Bruce Coville," *Something About the Author*, vol. 118, 36.

12 Bruce Coville's Interview Transcript.

13 Ibid.

14 Ibid.

15 Author Chats, "Read Across America Chat with Bruce Coville," March 2, 2001.

www.authorchats.com/archives/viewArchive.jsp?id=20010302 BruceCoville.jsp&t=Bruce+Coville.

16 Coville, *How I Got Here.*

17 Ibid.

18 Ibid.

19 Laura T. Ryan, "Labor in Cemetery Was Fear Antidote," *Syracuse Post-Standard*, February 10, 2003, F-13.

20 Ibid.

21 Ibid.

22 Bruce Coville's Interview Transcript.

23 Ibid.

24 Coville, *How I Got Here.*

25 Ibid.

26 Bruce Coville, *The Foolish Giant* (New York: HarperCollins, 1978), 21–22.

27 *Publisher's Weekly*, Jan. 19, 1990.

28 The Official Bruce Coville Site: Sarah's Unicorn, *www.brucecoville.com/books/2-sarah.htm.*

29 Author Chats, "Read Across America Chat with Bruce Coville," March 2, 2001.

30 Quoted in Anne Commire, ed., "Bruce Coville," *Something About the Author*, vol. 32 (Detroit, MI: Gale Research Company, 1983), 58.

31 Quoted in "Bruce Coville," *Contemporary Authors New Revision Series*, Vol. 96 (Farmington Hills, MI: Gale Group, 2001), 72.

32 Ibid.

33 Ibid.

34 Hal Marcovitz's interview with Bruce Coville, December 13, 2004.

35 Ibid.

36 Quoted in Anne Commire, ed., "Bruce Coville," *Something About the Author*, vol. 32 (Detroit, MI: Gale Research Company, 1983), 58.

37 Bruce Coville, *Into the Land of the Unicorns* (New York: Scholastic, 1994), 28.

38 Ibid., 68.

39 Ibid., 72.

40 Ibid., 61.

41 The Unicorn Chronicles, *www.theunicornchronicles.com/author.htm*.

42 Quoted in Jessica Lennan, Meghan Fitts, and Andrea Gaskin, "Talking with Bruce Coville," *Newsday*, June 13, 1995.

43 Coville, *Into the Land of the Unicorns*, 53.

44 Author Chats, "Read Across America Chat with Bruce Coville," March 2, 2001.

45 Ibid.

46 Bruce Coville's Interview Transcript.

47 Coville, *Into the Land of Unicorns*, 29.

48 Ibid., 30.

49 Bruce Coville's Interview Transcript.

50 Quoted in Paula W. Graham, *Speaking of Journals* (Honesdale, PA: Boyds Mill Press, 1999), 189.

51 Ibid., 191–192.

52 The Official Bruce Coville Site, *www.brucecoville.com/tips.htm*.

53 Bruce Coville's Interview Transcript.

54 Quoted in Graham, *Speaking of Journals*, 189.

55 Bruce Coville, *Aliens Ate My Homework* (New York: Simon & Schuster, 1993), 41.

56 Quoted in "Aliens Invaded His Brain: Bruce Coville is One Spacey Guy," *Time for Kids*, February 2, 1996.

57 Ibid.

58 Ibid.

59 Bruce Coville, *My Teacher is an Alien* (New York: Simon & Schuster, 1989), 22–24.

60 Hal Marcovitz's interview with Bruce Coville, December 13, 2004.

61 Quoted in Lennan, Fitts, and Gaskin, "Talking with Bruce Coville."

62 Coville, *My Teacher is an Alien*, 107.

63 Author Chats, "Read Across America Chat with Bruce Coville," March 2, 2001.

64 Ibid.

65 Coville, *Aliens Ate My Homework*, 19.

66 Ibid., 4.

67 Author Chats, "Read Across America Chat with Bruce Coville," March 2, 2001.

68 The Official Bruce Coville Site: Space Brat, *www.brucecoville.com/books/3-brat1.htm*.

69 "Space Brat," *Publishers Weekly*, July 27, 1992.

70 Hal Marcovitz's interview with Bruce Coville, December 13, 2004.

71 Cherrie D. Abbey, ed., "Bruce Coville," *Biography Today Author Series* (Detroit, MI: Omnigraphics, 2001), 45.

72 Bruce Coville, *I Was a Sixth Grade Alien* (New York: Simon & Schuster, 1999), 41.

73 Quoted in Laura T. Ryan, "Out of this World: Writer and Illustrator Blast Off with a 12-Book Series," *Syracuse Herald American*, September 29, 2003, p. 23.

74 Coville, *I Was a Sixth Grade Alien*, 117.

75 Author Chats, "Read Across America Chat with Bruce Coville," March 2, 2001.

76 William Shakespeare, *Tragedies/William Shakespeare* (New York: Alfred Knopf, 1992), 447–448.

77 Hal Marcovitz's interview with Bruce Coville, December 13, 2004.

78 Quoted in Lennan, Fitts and Gaskin, "Talking with Bruce Coville."

79 Bruce Coville, *William Shakespeare's Macbeth* (New York: Dial Books, 1997).

80 Ibid.

81 William Shakespeare, *Hamlet* (Baltimore, MD: Penguin Books, 1971), 151.

82 Bruce Coville, *Stages of Adaptation* [unpublished essay].

83 Bruce Coville, *Fortune's Journey* (Mahwah, NJ: BrideWater Paperbacks, 1997), 39.

84 Coville, *Stages of Adaptation*.

85 Ibid.

86 Hal Marcovitz's interview with Bruce Coville, December 13, 2004.

87 Coville, *Stages of Adaptation*.

88 Ibid.

89 William Shakespeare, *Tragedies/William Shakespeare*, 441.

90 Coville, *William Shakespeare's Macbeth*.

91 Coville, *Stages of Adaptation*.

92 Hal Marcovitz's interview with Bruce Coville, December 13, 2004.

93 William Shakespeare, *Tragedies/William Shakespeare*, 454.

94 Coville, *William Shakespeare's Macbeth*.

95 Quoted in Robin Tallis, ed., "Bruce Coville," *Something About the Author*, vol. 118, 38.

96 William Shakespeare, *Tragedies/William Shakespeare*, 520.

97 Coville, *William Shakespeare's Macbeth*.

98 Dawn Miller, "*Hamlet* for Fourth-Graders, Children's Author Stays True to Bard with Picture Books," *Charleston Gazette*, April 25, 2004, P-3.

99 Phyllis Fantauzzo, "Introducing Shakespeare," *Teaching Pre K-8* 34, no. 7 (2004), 84.

100 Coville, *Stages of Adaptation*.

101 The Official Bruce Coville Site: Armageddon Summer, *www.brucecoville.com/books/ 3-armageddon.htm*.

102 Hal Marcovitz's interview with Bruce Coville, December 13, 2004.

103 Jane Yolen and Bruce Coville, *Armageddon Summer* (New York: Harcourt, 1998), 81.

104 Ibid., 62–63.

105 Hal Marcovitz's interview with Bruce Coville, December 13, 2004.

106 Ibid.

107 Yolen and Coville, *Armageddon Summer*, 108.

108 The Official Bruce Coville Site: Armageddon Summer.

109 Ibid.

110 Ibid.

111 Ibid.

112 Ibid.

113 "Armageddon Summer," *Publishers Weekly*, June 15, 1998.

114 The Official Bruce Coville Site: Armageddon Summer.

115 Coville, *How I Got Here*.

116 Quoted in Jim McKeever, "Syracuse Author Faces Censorship," *Syracuse Post-Standard*, July 29, 1993, B-1.

117 Ibid.

118 Ibid.

119 Quoted in Jim McKeever, "Syracuse Author's Book Can Stay in School Library," *Syracuse Herald-Journal*, August 7, 1993, A-1.

120 Hal Marcovitz's interview with Bruce Coville, December 13, 2004.

121 Marion Dane Bauer, ed., *Am I Blue? Coming Out from the Silence* (New York: HarperCollins, 1994), 12–13.

122 Ibid., 16.

123 Hal Marcovitz's interview with Bruce Coville, December 13, 2004.

124 Quoted in Deidre Bello, "Parents Want Gay Literature Removed," *Iowa City Press-Citizen*, October 23, 2004.

125 Ibid.

126 Ibid.

127 Quoted in Deidre Bello, "Solon Debates Class Material," *Iowa City Press-Citizen*, October 27, 2004.

128 Quoted in Deidre Bello, "Solon Board OKs Gay Material," *Iowa City Press-Citizen*, November 11, 2004.

129 Hal Marcovitz's interview with Bruce Coville, December 13, 2004.

130 Between the Lines: Interview with Bruce Coville.

131 Ibid.

1950 Bruce Coville born May 16.

1962 Writes his first short story.

1967 Reads *Winnie-the-Pooh* by A.A. Milne and is inspired to write children's literature.

1968 Enrolls at Duke University, North Carolina; transfers to Harpur College (now part of State University of New York [SUNY] at Binghamton). Later transfers to SUNY Oswego, where he earns his bachelor's degree.

1969 Marries Katherine Dietz.

1974 Hired to teach at Wetzel Road Elementary School in Liverpool, New York.

1978 *The Foolish Giant* published.

1979 *Sarah's Unicorn* published.

1981 Leaves Wetzel Road Elementary School.

1982 *The Monster's Ring* published.

1983 Co-host and co-producer of *Upstage*, a cable-TV program promoting local theater in Syracuse, New York.

1987 *The Ghost in the Third Row* published.

1989 *My Teacher Is an Alien* published.

1991 *Jeremy Thatcher, Dragon Hatcher* published.

1992 *Space Brat* published.

1993 *Aliens Ate My Homework* and *William Shakespeare's The Tempest* published. Parents in Carroll, Iowa, argue *Jeremy Thatcher, Dragon Hatcher* promotes Satanism and witchcraft.

1994 *Into the Land of the Unicorns* published. Provides title story for *Am I Blue?: Coming Out from the Silence*, an anthology of gay literature.

1998 *Armageddon Summer* published.

1999 Establishes Full Cast Audio to produce unabridged audio versions of children's literature; *I Was a Sixth Grade Alien* published.

2004 Parents in Solon, Iowa, call for the removal of *Am I Blue?: Coming Out from the Silence* from an eighth-grade English class.

2005 Expected publication of *The Last Hunt* and *Thor's Wedding Day*.

ALIENS ATE MY HOMEWORK

This first book in the Rod Allbright Alien Adventures series finds 12-year-old Rod helping a group of intergalactic policemen capture a dangerous criminal.

ARMAGEDDON SUMMER

Written with Jane Yolen, *Armageddon Summer* tells the story of two teenagers, Marina and Jed, who are drawn into a cult by their parents. The cult leader, Reverend Beelson, has convinced his followers that the end of the world is near. He says their only chance of survival is to camp together on top of a mountain, surrounded by an electrified fence patrolled by armed guards.

THE GHOST IN THE THIRD ROW

Strange things start happening after Nina Tanleven tries out for a part in a play—scripts are ripped up, sets are knocked down, and a costume is torn to pieces Then Nina comes down with a genuine case of stage fright when she sees a ghost sitting in the third row of the theater. Through some detective work, Nina learns that the ghost, known as the Woman in White, was murdered in the theater 50 years ago.

INTO THE LAND OF THE UNICORNS

The first book in the series known as the Unicorn Chronicles finds Cara Diane crossing over from Earth into the Land of Luster, where she must deliver a magical amulet to Arabella Skydancer, queen of the unicorns.

I WAS A SIXTH GRADE ALIEN

Tim Tompkins has always considered himself to be the weirdest kid in class. That is until aliens from the planet Hevi-Hevi make contact with Earth and establish their embassy in Syracuse, New York. When the alien ambassador to Earth insists that his purple son, Pleskit Meenom, attend a normal elementary school in Syracuse, Pleskit joins Tim's class and Tim sees he is not so weird after all.

THE MONSTER'S RING

In the first of the five Magic Shop books, Russell Crannaker endures the tormenting of a bully named Eddie until he obtains a ring in Mr. Elives's Magic Shop that enables him to turn into a monster. Russell uses the ring to learn that Eddie is also the victim of bullies.

MY TEACHER IS AN ALIEN

Susan Simmons, Peter Thompson, and Duncan Dougal learn that their substitute teacher Mr. Smith is an alien with plans to kidnap five children for a trip into outer space. The three young people figure out a way to thwart his plans and save their real teacher, who has been taken captive by Smith.

SPACE BRAT

Blork is the biggest brat on the planet Splat. He may throw the biggest tantrums on the planet, but when the Big Pest Squad snatches his pet poodnoobie, Blork learns it will take more than a tantrum to get him back.

WILLIAM SHAKESPEARE'S MACBETH

William Shakespeare's Macbeth is one of six plays by William Shakespeare that Coville has retold in storybook form. Each book preserves a large measure of Shakespeare's poetry but enables the student to read the stories without plowing through blank verse, the style of sixteenth-century writing Shakespeare followed. *Macbeth* tells the story of murder and ambition in medieval Scotland.

I Was a Sixth Grade Alien series

1999 *I Was a Sixth Grade Alien, The Attack of the Two-Inch Teacher, I Lost My Grandfather's Brain*

2000 *Peanut Butter Lover Boy, Zombies of the Science Fair, Don, Too Many Aliens, Snatched from Earth, There's an Alien in My Backpack*

2001 *The Revolt of the Miniature Mutants, There's an Alien in My Underwear, Farewell to Earth*

Space Brat Series

1992 *Space Brat*

1993 *Space Brat 2: Blork's Evil Twin*

1994 *Space Brat 3: The Wrath of Squat*

1995 *Space Brat 4: The Planet of the Dips*

1997 *Space Brat 5: The Saber-Toothed Poodnoobie*

Rod Allbright Alien Adventures Series

1993 *Aliens Ate My Homework*

1994 *I Left My Sneakers in Dimension X*

1995 *The Search for Snout*

1998 *Aliens Stole My Body*

Magic Shop Series

1982 *The Monster's Ring*

1991 *Jeremy Thatcher, Dragon Hatcher; Jennifer Murdley's Toad*

1997 *The Skull of Truth*

2003 *Juliet Dove, Queen of Love*

Nina Tanleven Stories

1987 *The Ghost in the Third Row, The Ghost Wore Gray*

1991 *The Ghost in the Big Brass Bed*

The A.I. Gang Stories

1986 *A.I. Gang: Forever Begins Tomorrow; A.I. Gang: Operation Sherlock*

1995 *A.I. Gang: Robot Trouble*

The Unicorn Chronicles

1994 *Into the Land of the Unicorns*

1999 *Song of the Wanderer*

Anthologies

1989 *Herds of Thunder, Manes of Gold*

1998 *A Glory of Unicorns*

Camp Haunted Hills Series

1988 *How I Survived My Summer Vacation*

1989 *Some of My Best Friends Are Monsters*

1990 *The Dinosaur that Followed Me Home*

Bruce Coville's Book of . . . Series

1995 *Bruce Coville's Book of Aliens, Bruce Coville's Book of Monsters, Bruce Coville's Book of Ghosts, Bruce Coville's Book of Nightmares*

1996 *Bruce Coville's Book of Spine-Tinglers, Bruce Coville's Book of Magic, Bruce Coville's Book of Monsters II, Bruce Coville's Book of Aliens II*

1997 *Bruce Coville's Book of Spine-Tinglers II, Bruce Coville's Book of Ghosts II, Bruce Coville's Book of Magic II, Bruce Coville's Book of Nightmares II*

My Teacher Is an Alien Series

1989 *My Teacher is an Alien*

1991 *My Teacher Fried My Brains, My Teacher Glows in the Dark*

1992 *My Teacher Flunked the Planet*

Shakespeare Retellings Series

1993 *William Shakespeare's The Tempest*

1996 *William Shakespeare's A Midsummer Night's Dream*

1997 *William Shakespeare's Macbeth*

1999 *William Shakespeare's Romeo and Juliet*

2003 *William Shakespeare's Twelfth Night*

2004 *William Shakespeare's Hamlet*

Young Adult Novels

1995 *Fortune's Journey*

1996 *Space Station Ice-3*

1998 *Armageddon Summer*

Chamber of Horrors Series

1996 *Amulet of Doom, Spirits and Spells, Eyes of the Tarot, Waiting Spirits*

Picture Books

1979 *The Foolish Giant*

1979 *Sarah's Unicorn*

1984 *Sarah and the Dragon*

1997 *My Grandfather's House, The Lapsnatcher*

2002 *The Prince of Butterflies*

Oddities Series

1997 *Oddly Enough*

2000 *Odder Than Ever*

Middle Grade Novels

1989 *Monster of the Year*

1992 *Goblins in the Castle*

1996 *The World's Worst Fairy Godmother*

1994 *The Dragonslayers*

2003 *The Monsters of Morley Manor*

BLORK

Blork, the main character in *Space Brat* and other books in the series, learns that throwing temper tantrums won't get him what he wants on the planet Splat.

CARA DIANE

Cara Diane, a young girl from Earth, crosses the bridge into the Land of Luster with the help of a magical amulet. Her adventures find her saving the unicorns in *Into the Land of the Unicorns* and *Song of the Wanderer*.

JED AND MARINA

Jed and Marina, the two young protagonists in *Armageddon Summer*, arrive at the mountaintop camp of the Church of the Believers with different ideas about what they are doing there. Marina is looking for a reason to believe that the end of the world is coming, while Jed is convinced that Reverend Beelson's prediction of an Armageddon is bunk.

MR. ELIVES

Mr. Elives is the proprietor of a magic shop who finds just the right item for the troubled young people who wander through his doors, including Jeremy Thatcher in *Jeremy Thatcher, Dragon Hatcher*; Juliet Dove in *Juliet Dove, Queen of Love*; Jennifer Mudley in *Jennifer Mudley's Toad*; Charlie Eggleston in *The Skull of Truth*; and Russell Crannaker in *The Monster's Ring*.

NINA TANLEVEN

Aspiring actress Nina Tanleven is the main character in three books by Bruce Coville, including *The Ghost in the Third Row*, which draws Nina into the mystery surrounding a murdered actress.

PLESKIT MEENOM AND TIM TOMPKINS

Pleskit Meenom, a purple boy from the planet Hevi-Hevi, and Tim Tompkins, a sixth-grader from Syracuse, New York, join forces for adventures in the 12-book series that started with *I Was a Sixth Grade Alien*.

ROD ALLBRIGHT

Bruce Coville based the character of 12-year-old Rod Allbright on himself, making Rod the main character in a series of books that commenced with *Aliens Ate My Homework*, in which Rod helps a group of intergalactic policemen capture a feared criminal.

SUSAN SIMMONS, PETER THOMPSON, AND DUNCAN DOUGAL

Readers first meet Susan Simmons, Peter Thompson, and Duncan Dougal in *My Teacher Is an Alien* as they thwart the alien Broxholm's plans to kidnap five children from Earth. They return as main characters in three more books in the series.

1982 *The Monster's Ring*, selected for the International Reading Association Children's Choice List.

1983 *Sarah and the Dragon*, selected for the International Reading Association Children's Choice List.

1986 *Operation Sherlock*, selected for the International Reading Association Children's Choice List.

1989 *Herds of Thunder, Manes of Gold*, selected by the New York Public Library as a Book for the Teen Age.

1991 *Jeremy Thatcher, Dragon Hatcher*, selected for the International Reading Association Children's Choice List. *My Teacher Glows in the Dark*, wins the first Golden Duck Award for best children's science fiction book.

1994 *Oddly Enough*, selected by the American Library Association as a Best Book for Young Adults and named to the association's Quick Pick List.

1997 *William Shakespeare's Macbeth*, named to the American Library Association's Quick Pick List. *The Skull of Truth*, selected by the School Library Journal as Best Book of the Year. Bruce Coville received the Knickerbocker Award from the New York Library Association for his entire body of work.

1998 *Armageddon Summer*, selected by the American Library Association as a Best Book for Young Adults and named to the association's Quick Pick List. Also selected by Voice of Youth Advocates as an Outstanding Title.

1999 *Odder Than Ever*, named to the Voice of Youth Advocates Best Science Fiction, Fantasy and Horror List. *I Was a Sixth Grade Alien*, wins the Golden Duck Award for best children's science fiction book. *William Shakespeare's Romeo and Juliet*, selected by the American Library Association for its Quick Pick List.

2003 *William Shakespeare's Twelfth Night*, selected by the Parents' Choice Foundation for the Silver Honor Award, and named to the Book of the Year List by Bank Street College. Bruce Coville awarded an honorary doctorate degree from the State University of New York at Oswego.

Abbie, Cherrie D., ed. "Bruce Coville." *Biography Today Author Series*. Detroit, MI: Omnigraphics, 2001.

"Aliens Invaded His Brain: Bruce Coville is One Spacey Guy," *Time for Kids*, February 2, 1996.

Author Chats. "Read Across America Chat with Bruce Coville." *www.authorchats.com/archives/viewArchive.jsp?id=20010302 BruceCoville.jsp&t=Bruce+Coville*.

Bello, Deidre. "Parents Want Gay Literature Removed." *Iowa City Press-Citizen*, October 23, 2004.

Bello, Deidre. "Solon Board OKs Gay Material." *Iowa City Press-Citizen*, November 11, 2004.

Bello, Deidre. "Solon Debates Class Material." *Iowa City Press-Citizen*, October 27, 2004.

"Between the Lines: Interview with Bruce Coville." *www.harcourtbooks.com/authorinterviews/bookinterview_Coville.asp*.

"Bruce Coville's Interview Transcript ." www2.scholastic.com/teachers/authorsandbooks/authorstudies/author home.jhtml;schsessionid=IADLNRYFM5CGKCQVAKUCF-FAKCUBJYIV4?authorID=22&collateralID=5327&displayName= Interview+Transcript.

Commire, Anne, ed. *Something About the Author* Vol. 32. Detroit, MI: Gale Research Co., 1983.

Coville, Bruce. "The Name Game." *Writing* 25, no. 5 (February–March 2003).

Coville, Bruce. "Stages of Adaptation." Unpublished essay on retelling the plays of William Shakespeare.

Fantauzzo, Phyllis. "Introducing Shakespeare." *Teaching Pre K–8* 34, no. 7 (April 1, 2004).

Graham, Paula W. *Speaking of Journals*. Honesdale, PA: Boyds Mill Press, 1999.

Hile, Kevin S. and Diane Telgen, ed. *Something About the Author* Vol. 77. Detroit, MI: Gale Research Inc., 1994.

Jordan, Anne. "The Monster's Ring." *New York Times Book Review*, October 31, 1982.

Lennan, Jessica, Meghan Fitts, and Andrea Gaskin. "Talking with Bruce Coville." *Newsday*, June 13, 1995.

Locher, Frances C., ed. *Contemporary Authors* Vols. 97–100. Detroit, MI: Gale Research Co., 1981.

McKeever, Jim. "Syracuse Author Faces Censorship." *Syracuse Post-Standard*, July 29, 1993.

McKeever, Jim. "Syracuse Author's Book Can Stay in School Library." *Syracuse-Post Standard*, August 7, 1993.

Miller, Dawn. "*Hamlet* for Fourth-Graders, Children's Author Stays True to Bard with Picture Books." *Charleston Gazette*, April 25, 2004.

Myrick, Ellen. "The In-side Story: I Was a Rat at Full Cast Audio." *www.ingramlibrary.com/nwsltr/september03/ILS_insidestory.html*.

Ryan, Laura T. "Labor in Cemetery Was Fear Antidote." *Syracuse Post-Standard*, February 10, 2003.

Ryan, Laura T. "Out of this World: Writer and Illustrator Blast Off with a 12-Book Series." *Syracuse Herald American*, September 29, 2003.

Straub, Deborah, ed. *Contemporary Authors New Revision Series* Vol. 22. Detroit, MI: Gale Research Company, 1988.

Tallis, Robyn. "Bruce Coville," *Contemporary Authors New Revision Series* Vol. 96. Farmington Hills, MI: Gale Group, 2001.

Tallis, Robyn. "Bruce Coville," *Something About the Author* Vol. 118. Farmington Hills, MI: Gale Group, 2001.

"Two Schools Make Censorship List." *Lancaster Intelligencer-Journal*, August 31, 1995.

Campbell, Joseph. *The Hero with a Thousand Faces*. Princeton, NJ: Princeton University Press, 2004.

Graham, Paula W. *Speaking of Journals*. Honesdale, PA: Boyds Mill Press, 1999.

Graves, Robert. *The Greek Myths*. Kingston, RI: Moyer Bell, 2004.

———. *The Hebrew Myths*. New York: Random House, 1986.

———. *The White Goddess*. Manchester, England: Carcanet Press, 1999.

Milne, A.A. *The Complete Tales of Winnie-the-Pooh*. New York: Dutton Children's Books, 1994.

www.brucecoville.com
> *[Bruce Coville's Official Internet site. Visitors to Bruce
> Coville's official Internet site can read interviews with the
> author and excerpts from his books. A schedule of Coville's
> personal appearances at bookstores, libraries, and schools is
> listed. Fans who submit drawings of Coville's characters may
> see them posted on the site. Also, Coville offers writing tips for
> young authors and provides links to some of his favorite
> authors' sites. Posted on the site is an interview with Coville
> and Jane Yolen that focuses on their work on* Armageddon
> Summer. *The interview first appeared as a story in* Book Links,
> *the magazine of the American Library Association.]*

http://theunicornchronicles.com/
> *[Website for the Bruce Coville's Unicorn Chronicles series.
> Bruce Coville maintains this web page to provide excerpts
> and updates for the books in the Unicorn Chronicles series.
> By entering the word "unicorn" in an Internet search engine,
> students can find dozens of web resources that tell the myths
> and stories associated with unicorns.]*

www.ala.org/ala/oif/bannedbooksweek/bannedbooksweek.htm
> *[Official web page for the American Library Association's
> Banned Books Week. Banned Books Week is scheduled annually
> for the last week in September. Libraries and booksellers partic-
> ipate by prominently displaying, either for lending or for sale,
> the books that have been taken out of classroom, school, and
> public library shelves throughout the country. Entering the
> terms "banned books" or "book censorship" into an Internet
> search engine can provide the student with many on-line
> resources on the issue.]*

http://pages.prodigy.net/kas9865/
> *[Website about ghosts found in central New York maintained by
> the Syracuse Ghost Hunters.]*

www.folkstory.com/campbell/campbell.html
> *[Website on Joseph Campbell maintained by the California-
> based Center for Story and Symbol. Many other individuals
> and groups have made interpretations of Campbell's work
> available on-line, and they can be found by entering
> Campbell's name in an Internet search engine.]*

http://faculty.ed.umuc.edu/~rschumak/focus.htm
[On-line biography of poet Robert Graves maintained by the University of Maryland.]

http://library.brandeis.edu/about/nsf/kozol/biography.html
[Biography of Jonathan Kozol maintained by Brandeis University.]

www.rickross.com
[Website of the Rick A. Ross Institute of New Jersey with an extensive on-line archive of news stories about cults in America.]

HAL MARCOVITZ is a journalist who lives in Pennsylvania with his wife Gail and daughters Ashley and Michelle. He is the author of the satirical novel *Painting the White House* as well as more than 60 nonfiction books for young readers. His other titles in the WHO WROTE THAT? series include biographies of Will Hobbs and R.L. Stine.